THE
PERFECT
STOCK MARKET
DIET

THE PERFECT STOCK MARKET DIET

One Simple Strategy to Beat Wallstreet Professionals

GENE NADLER

Redwood Publishing, LLC
Orange County, California

First Printing, 2020

Printed in the United States of America

ISBN: 978-1-952106-36-1 (hardcover)
ISBN: 978-1-952106-37-8 (paperback)
ISBN: 978-1-952106-38-5 (ebook)

Library of Congress Control Number: 2020907468

Published by Redwood Publishing, LLC
Orange County, California
www.redwooddigitalpublishing.com
info@redwooddigitalpublishing.com

Disclaimer: This book is designed to provide information and motivation to its readers. It is sold with the understanding that the author and publisher are not engaged to render any type of psychological, legal, or any other kind of professional advice. The content of each article is the sole expression and opinion of its author and it not meant to substitute for any advice from your healthcare professionals, lawyers, therapists, business advisors/partners, or personal connections. The information provided in this book is designed to provide helpful information on the subjects discussed. Neither the author nor the publisher shall be held liable or responsible to any person or entity with respect to any loss or incidental or consequential damages caused, or alleged to have been caused, directly or indirectly, by the information contained herein.

Interior Design: Ghislain Viau
Cover Design: Michelle Manley

To Dr. Kevin Cahill for his encouragement.

Contents

Jack Bogle, with his invention of index investing, has made more money for more investors than anyone in history.
—Warren Buffett

When I told my accountant that I was writing a book
he asked if there would be a lot of sex and gore.
I told him that since it's a book about the stock market
there will be very little sex but gore a plenty.

CHAPTER 1

Your Financial Advisor Should Have a Warning Label: "My Advice May Be Injurious to Your Financial Health!"

This is going to be the most exciting book about investing in the stock market you've ever read, because I'm going to show you the secret of investing successfully—a secret that nobody on Wall Street wants you to know about.

At the same time, the approach I'll share with you may seem awfully boring, because the way to make real money in the stock market is far less exciting than the hype you see when you watch those addictive financial news cable channels, read the financial press, or go on websites about the stock market.

Right now, if you are like most investors, you are paying for a lot of useless advice. Your financial advisor almost certainly means well and is doing everything he or she can to serve you in an honest manner. But the sad reality is that over the long haul, 94 percent of financial advisors or portfolio managers fail to create returns for their clients that keep pace with the market. (By the market, I mean the S&P 500 index.) Ninety-four percent! That's almost nineteen out of twenty investment advisors! They all fall short. Okay, one lucky one beats the market, and every advisor believes that he or she will be that fortunate—but 94 percent of the time, they aren't. And on top of that, you are annually paying approximately 1 percent of your hard-earned wealth as a fee—for them to make you less money!

It sounds absurd when you describe it this way. And yet, millions upon millions of investors this year, next year, and the year after that will settle for less-than-optimal returns on their investments, and they will actually pay people to generate those less-than-optimal returns.

Although we've never met, I can say with great confidence that you, my new friend, are one of those people. My intention in these pages is to lay out for you exactly why so many investors do things that are completely contrary to their best possible stock market return, whether it's paying an investment advisor, or trying to pick individual stocks or time the market.

People do these things every day because they have been trained to do them. It is in the interest of the investment firms, financial news television networks, and most investment-oriented websites to keep you exactly where you are, making less money than you could make, turning over increasingly meaningful chunks of your wealth as fees, making bad bets, and putting your trust where it does not belong.

Ideally, you just need a couple of paragraphs to understand what you need to do in order to come out ahead of 94 percent of those well-dressed, well-spoken financial advisors who, in truth, don't know anything more about the market than you do. But it's going to take a whole book to explain the psychology of investing that most people—including you, most likely—have bought into. Unfortunately, this is the only investing methodology that anyone ever talks about.

Watch a football game and you'll see a dozen ads for financial services firms. Go online and you'll be bombarded with ads, articles, videos, and social media posts, all pointing you in the direction of an investing model that punishes investors instead of rewarding them. It's everywhere.

It all comes down to this: the investment houses are paying tens of millions of dollars every year for advertising to convince you that they know more about the market than you do, and that you should trust them to invest your money because they will do a better job than you ever could.

Other entities, like Jim Cramer (about whom you will learn plenty in this book), want to keep you pinballing from stock to stock, buying and selling, buying and selling. They get to sound brilliant, and you get to feel like you're on the inside of something that's going to make you a lot of money.

People like Cramer are trying to sell you the idea that you can do a little bit of homework, find a hot stock, and ride it up for fantastic gains. As long as you feel that way, you'll be playing right into their hands, buying and selling, buying and selling, but not getting anywhere in terms of maximizing your potential gains. These individuals, networks, and websites make a ton of money by convincing you that you only have to know a tiny bit about a company in order to profit handsomely—and quickly.

And then every so often, along comes a fraudster like Bernie Madoff or Charles Ponzi. Such a person is often able to convince thousands of people that they have special insight, special hedging skills, or special insider knowledge that allows them to make incredible returns year after year.

Why do people invest with fraudsters? Why do people believe that they can beat the market by betting on individual stocks that they don't know that much about? Why do people turn their money over to financial advisors who have no better an idea what's going to happen in the market tomorrow than you or I?

In two words: fear and greed.

Everybody's afraid of making a mistake, because no matter how "risk-tolerant" we may say we are, we don't want to lose a dime of our money. We want guaranteed upsides and no downsides. In fact, most of us would willingly accept a much lower upside if we could only have some guarantee that we won't lose much money when the market goes down. And when you really think about it, this is the pitch investment advisors make. They aren't saying, "We're going to make you a ton of money!" What they're really saying is, "If you come with us, you probably won't lose as much as the other guy when the market goes down." They don't put those exact words into their sales pitch, of course, because no one would ever invest with them. But that's essentially the message their advertising and marketing send.

As the old Woody Allen line goes, "A stockbroker is someone who invests your money until there's nothing left."

So that's the fear side of the equation—everybody's so afraid of making a mistake that they end up diminishing their own ability to maximize their returns.

Greed, of course, is the flip side of fear when it comes to market psychology. Greed drives people to think that they, as individuals, can outthink and outperform that massive institution called Wall Street. They watch a little Jim Cramer, they read a little Motley Fool, and before you know it, they think they're Warren Buffett. They hear a couple of things about a stock and they throw their money at it, hoping to capture that big move upward. Half the time, they don't even know what the company does! To them, the stock isn't an ownership percentage of a real, live company that employs people and makes real things or provides real services. It's just a piece of paper. They're buying a piece of paper for ten dollars and hoping the value of that piece of paper goes to fifty dollars.

Greed is the driver of the mentality that floods people's brains when they go to casinos or to the racetrack, or when they make bets on sporting events: "I'm smarter than the other guy. I'm smarter than the whole world, and I'll make a ton of money. Wait and see."

You go to the proverbial cocktail party and people are only talking about their wins. Everybody wants to look like a genius. But the real geniuses are not the people who hear a couple of things about a stock and throw money at it. The real geniuses are the ones who run the investment firms, who have the TV shows, and who own the websites . . . not because they have more financial acumen than the rest of us—they don't—but because they've figured out how to monetize the fear and greed of the average individual. That's a form of genius, wouldn't you agree?

So why do people do these things? Why do people turn their money over to investment advisors, invest in individual stocks about which they don't know all that much, and even do business with the Bernie Madoffs of the world? Why do people put their money with investment advisors? The simple answer is that the investment firms have spent huge amounts of money convincing you that they know more than you do about investing. If you don't trust your own judgment, they make money. And while they will always make money, there is no guarantee that you will.

Let's put it this way: For the last century, the market has returned 10 percent annually on a compounded basis. Along the way, it's gone down and it's gone up, so that if you look at any given day since 1920, you could be up a lot or down a lot—but in the long run it has provided an excellent return.

Is it the job of the financial advisor or money manager to make you the most money? No. It's the job of financial advisor to keep your money with him. The financial advisor who has the most money under his management is the most successful one, not the one who makes the most money for his clients. They're not even trying to make you the most money. As I said earlier, their goal is to make sure that if the market goes down a lot, you won't lose as much as other people. If the market goes up a lot, your advisor looks like a genius. If the market goes down a lot, and your person has kept you from the absolute worst, rock-bottom returns that some other people are getting, your advisor still looks like a genius.

But did they beat the market over the long term? No. As I said earlier—and this is a fact that every investor has to take to heart—94 percent of advisors, over the long term, fail to beat the market.

This means that if the market is up 10 percent annually over a fifteen-year period, 94 percent of advisors made less money for their clients. Nine percent. Eight percent. Seven percent. You're still up, so you still feel good. But not only did you fail to keep up with the market; you actually had to pay a 1 percent fee every year to your advisor . . . to get returns that are worse than the market itself! It's crazy! You're paying out good money (and over time *a lot* of good money) to someone who failed to get you the same returns that you could've gotten if you had just bought an investment on your own that represented the stock market. We'll talk about what those are shortly, but they exist—and 94 percent of advisors don't do as well as index-based investments.

Nevertheless, practically every investor happily pays 1 percent to financial advisors to get them, nineteen out of twenty times, lower returns than they could've gotten on their own with an investment in a fund that mimics the S&P. That's the long and short of the most successful stock market investment that the vast—I repeat, vast—majority of investors can make.

It's incredible—people actually pay fees to get worse results! What a world! So why do they do it?

Investment advisors, by and large, are honest people. They really believe that they're going to get you better results.

They don't go into the business because they want to steal from people. They want to help people. I should know—I was a financial advisor at Morgan Stanley for thirty-five years. I got to know hundreds, maybe thousands of financial advisors over the course of my career. Were they nice people? Were they honest? Did they want to do right by their clients? Absolutely! But the system they're in simply does not permit them to maximize returns for their clients. There is no direct alignment among the interests of the investment firm itself, the advisor, and the client. The investment firms consistently put their own interests first, and the investment advisors and stockbrokers are caught in the middle. They may not like the system, but they have to work in it.

So how do they justify their fees?

It used to be that they got paid every time you made a trade, so they were incentivized to make a lot of trades on your account. Sometimes they would make too many trades. This was called "churning," and it was totally inappropriate. Most advisors did not churn . . . but if they did not create enough business in their clients' accounts, they would get a phone call or a visit from their manager, who would want to know what was going on. Nobody likes getting those kinds of calls or visits, so they would make trades, which generated fees for the advisors and for the investment firms. Were the trades necessarily in the best interest of the clients? Sometimes yes, sometimes no. But of all the entities in this equation—the investment firm, the investment advisor, and the client—the client came in last.

Today, things have changed. We're moving to an environment where the cost of making trades has gone from high to low to zero. Today you can go to a variety of online platforms and buy and sell stocks, funds, or whatever, with no fees. So, since those fees have either diminished or vanished, advisors have had to figure out a different model in order to make a living. So they now charge a fee, typically 1 percent, on all the money you invest with them.

One percent. Doesn't sound like very much, does it? I mean, if you heard that your favorite store was offering a 1 percent sale, would you hurry over there? Of course not! If you heard that your tax rate was going up 1 percent, would you call your congressman and throw a fit? You wouldn't even notice. You'd just say, "I'm lucky to live in a free country, and if I have to pay one more percent, so be it."

That's the genius of the investment firms moving to a model of charging investors 1 percent. It sounds like nothing. Who's going to make a big deal out of 1 percent? The only problem is that 1 percent of your money, year after year after year, adds up. In fact, because of compound interest, it adds up *a lot* as time goes by. This is money that should've been in your pocket. It should've remained in your investments, so it could've made you more money. But instead, the money went into the pockets of the investment advisors and the investment firms. That's how they can afford those beautiful offices. They're using your money to pay for them.

So what do advisors do to keep people happy? Many take what is described as a "holistic" approach: They aren't just offering you investment advice; they're having chocolate fondue nights. They're sponsoring dinners where you can come and enjoy a nice meal and hear from "experts" about where the market is headed. (I put the word *experts* in quotes because there's no such thing as an expert on the future.)

They'll do more than that: When your daughter gets married, they'll come to her wedding. Isn't that nice? Can you imagine—your financial advisor is taking an evening out of his life to come to *your* daughter's wedding! You feel great about that, right? Isn't he thoughtful? I'll tell you what he is—he's smart as hell! You're going to introduce him to all your friends, so he's going to be able to give out a lot of business cards. Your daughter and her husband are going to be so touched that he showed up that they are likely to keep the same advisor, in your lifetime and after you're gone. Is it still nice that the advisor came to the wedding? Of course it is . . . but let's get real. This is part of the business.

When the market goes down, your financial advisor is a shoulder to cry on. You're getting divorced? Chances are, your financial advisor will know before your best friend, your divorce attorney, or even your spouse. They take on the role of best friend, psychologist, and confidante. If you're thinking about getting a new car, before you call the Tesla dealer, you call your investment advisor. Should I buy or lease? New or pre-owned? Why *shouldn't* you call them? They encourage you to pick up the phone. They want to hear from you about these things. Because the more services they offer, the more likely you are to stick with them and keep paying them that 1 percent—even though 94 percent of the time, they're getting beaten by the market.

Investment advisors are paid 1 percent of all the money they manage. They never get paid for the value they add by an outperformance of the market, for a simple reason: They do not add value to the return of the S&P index. No value added would mean no fees. Buy the index. Skip the fees. Get and keep more money in your investment for yourself.

Think about how much money you have with your financial advisor. How much is 1 percent of that? In other words, how much are you paying in fees each year? Is it really worth all that money to have somebody come to your daughter's wedding and tell you whether you should buy or lease the Tesla? You could pay a total stranger to come to your daughter's wedding for maybe $250. You could hire a therapist for five hours to talk about whether you should get divorced. And quite frankly, at your income level, it really doesn't matter all that much whether you buy or lease—enjoy yourself; it's just a car.

And yet, most of us are content to pay our advisors tens of thousands of dollars for "advice," and for their consolation and warmth when our marriage tanks, or when the market goes down and we just need a little bit of reassurance. That's "holistic" investment advice. We feel so warm and fuzzy that we barely notice that they're taking all these fees for getting us subpar results.

Now let's talk about individual stocks.

Why is it that everybody thinks that they're so smart? The simple, painful reality is this: Most people who pick individual stocks fail to beat the market as a whole. In other words, if you compare the portfolio of a hundred, a hundred thousand, or a million investors who buy and sell individual stocks over any period of time, you will find that inevitably they come up short. This sounds so hard to believe because the Jim Cramers of the world make it seem so easy. He runs around his set, he shouts, he makes noises, and you sit there thinking, "I could do that! I could ride the upside on that stock! Why not me?"

It all comes back to what I said earlier—the stock-picking mentality has people believing that stocks are not real companies. They're just pieces of paper.

Let's think for a second. How many people can you name who have successfully beaten the market over a meaningful period of time. I'll wait. How many?

Warren Buffett? Of course. But there's only one Warren Buffett. Are you going to be the next Warren Buffett?

Peter Lynch? Good answer. Peter Lynch was the fund manager at Fidelity's Magellan Fund, and for many years, Lynch, in fact, beat the market. He chose individual stocks the same way Warren Buffett did, and the same way I have. He wrote a book about it called *Beating the Street*, in which he made it sound easy—but just because it's easy doesn't mean, as they say on TV, that you should try this at home.

Peter Lynch and the Magellan Fund eventually became victims of their own success. The more successful the fund got and the more famous Lynch became, the more money started sloshing into the fund. In fact, so much money came in that there were few companies in which he could invest the money without distorting the stock price for that company. So eventually, even the vaunted Magellan Fund started to underperform for its investors. Yes, Peter Lynch beat the market, but for a very short time—less than fifteen years.

Even Warren Buffett says that he couldn't be the Warren Buffett of old in today's world. There's just too much money chasing too few opportunities. Buffett will tell you, in his annual reports and in his speeches, that there's no way even an individual as experienced as he is could find enough investment opportunities to create the same kind of returns that his company, Berkshire Hathaway, created in decades past, with his amount of wealth.

Let me tell you about one other individual who actually found a couple of stocks and beat the market with them: me.

Yes, the same person who's telling you not to try this yourself actually *was* successful—not just once, but twice—at picking individual stocks and clobbering the market. I'll tell you those stories more fully in Chapter 2, but I'll give you a taste right now: It was a company called SodaStream, I liked their product, I did my homework, I invested in it, and I made a lot of money. Same thing with Timberland boots.

So here I am telling you that investing in individual stocks usually doesn't work . . . and yet also telling you that I did it twice.

The one thing I'm not telling you is that I did it a third time. You know why? Because I've never found a third company that I could get behind the way I was able to get behind Soda-Stream and Timberland. These were absolutely one-of-a-kind experiences for me. Would I love to find a third stock? Of course! But in the years since I made all that money on those two companies, have I found one more? No, I haven't. And who knows? I may never find that third company.

I didn't do what most people do. Most people watch guys like Jim Cramer, or they get a tip on a "hot stock" at a cocktail party, and they throw money at that stock. That's not how I did it. I put more than two thousand hours of research into each of those two companies. That's what was necessary for me to invest my money and my clients' money in those companies in good conscience.

A guy like Jim Cramer would never tell you that you need to put two thousand hours into a company. All they tell you is, "This company is going up, throw your money at it, and good luck." To me, that sounds a lot more like gambling than investing. I'm here to tell you that you might as well go to Vegas and play craps than try to pick individual stocks and beat the market. Peter Lynch did it dozens of times. Warren Buffett did it countless times. I had the amazing good fortune to do it twice.

But you're not Warren Buffett. What are the chances that you are going to spend half an hour reading about a company, hit the buy button, and make a fortune? I don't like your chances, and frankly, neither should you. In the next chapter, I'll share with you my background, and I'll show you how I beat the market not just once, but twice. I'm not trying to show off. Instead, I just want to illustrate for you how hard it is to pull off this feat. With that dose of reality, you may be open to my ideas for how to make the maximum return in the stock market when others are failing to get similar results. It may be not be the sexiest, most exciting approach to investing, but getting great returns is much more exciting than the ups and downs that most investors experience. And that's why I've written this book.

CHAPTER 2

How I Beat the Market . . . Twice (But Don't Try This at Home!)

If you are going to put all your eggs in one basket,
you'd better be very sure of that basket.
—Warren Buffett

I was always fascinated by the stock market. From the time I was eleven years old, it appeared magical to me, because you were dealing with money that, as far as I could tell, you didn't have to work for. What eleven-year-old *wouldn't* find that amazing? I admit that I was laboring under a preadolescent delusion, but at the time, it was exciting.

Back then, I would be out with a couple of friends—my mother would toss me out of the house for the day—and we would sit on the stairs in Bloomingdale's with a copy of the *New York Times* that I had bought. I would give the entertainment section to my friend, who was a budding musician, and I would give the sports section to my other friend, who was a jock. Me? I would read the financial section. And when I say I read it, I mean I spent over an hour reading it carefully. All those facts and figures, the columns of numbers in agate type, all the stories of stocks reaching new highs—it lit a fire in me.

I was not a typical eleven-year-old.

My father worked in the garment center, specifically the ready-to-wear business, and when I became an adult, I worked with him for about four years. I loved my dad, but I really had no interest in continuing to work with him or to stay in the garment industry—I still loved the stock market.

So I got a job at EF Hutton as a retail broker. From the first day, I knew I was where I belonged. I was good at mathematical concepts, and I think the firm recognized that fairly early. I met Bob Shulman, who was in charge of options for the brokers in the tristate area. He would lecture us on options, and I found him fascinating.

He was also my first professional exposure to risk management. Options can be speculative, but you can also use them to manage risk. During my training at Hutton, there were at least fifteen or twenty people who taught us various topics. But Shulman by far stood out as the most interesting and the most mathematically analytical in his thinking. I'd like to say we were kindred spirits.

My training period lasted about six months, and then they gave me a desk and a phone and told me to start making calls. As a retail broker, my job was to cold-call. I would get on the phone with a total stranger and say, "Hi, my name is Gene Nadler, I'm with EF Hutton, and I want to tell you about a utility stock that yields 6 percent . . . and it's tax advantaged." Back then, certain utility stocks paid out their dividends with certain tax advantages so that the dividends would be taxed as capital gains instead of as regular income. That made a big difference at that time, the early 1980s.

This is what I did all day long—call people up and tell them the same story, over and over, about the stock I was pitching.

What's it like to cold-call? It's constant repetition and constant rejection. It was hard work, but over time I was able to build up a clientele. My sales pitch was very conservative, and people seemed to trust me. Maybe it wasn't quite as glamorous as I had imagined when I was an eleven-year-old reading the stock pages on the steps of Bloomingdale's with my friends—but at least I was on the inside.

In my group of five newbie brokers, there was one guy whom I would call a super salesman. Back then, most of us would be opening ten accounts a month, but he was opening forty or fifty. We found out that he was selling a bond from the Federal Farm Credit Bank, a federal agency. Yields on the bond back then were very high, maybe 14 or 15 percent, with a federal guarantee. That was a fabulous thing to offer if you were trying to open accounts.

The only problem was that within a year the rate had dropped to 10 percent, but he was still selling it as a bond that yielded 15 percent. As you can imagine, that led to terrible problems. What he was doing wasn't that different from what Madoff did. He was making promises that people should've known weren't possible to keep. As you can imagine, once they found out, he didn't last long, and they had to unwind all those deals he had made.

I wasn't flashy or super salesy like that guy (and on top of that, I was honest). I was more like the tortoise than the hare. But I kept at it, and gradually grew my business.

Throughout my first fifteen years, I consistently trailed the market. It was frustrating. I never sold anything I didn't believe in; I just had no idea what the things I was selling were, or what they were worth. (It's extremely lucky that I never had any success with those investments, because if I had, I might have started to think that I was some sort of genius or something!) I made gains for my clients and myself—I always put my money into anything I suggested for my clients; that seemed like the ethical thing to do—but I was never able to create returns that met the market. I didn't realize that this was the case for 94 percent of professionals, as we discussed in the previous chapter. I just thought maybe I wasn't that good. I wasn't that bad, but clearly I wasn't anything to write home about.

And then one day in 1993, something changed. I was shopping for shoes, and I found a pair I really liked. They were water-resistant, and they looked great and felt great. I asked the salesman, "What's the brand of this shoe?" He told me they were Timberlands, and I bought them immediately.

Back then, Peter Lynch, who ran the famous Fidelity Magellan Fund, was preaching that you ought to invest in things close at hand that you knew something about. I had a background in the garment business, thanks to my father, so I knew a nice piece of apparel when I saw one.

So I started to delve into the financials of the company. The numbers were decent. Timberland wasn't super profitable back then, but they were growing, and most intriguingly, I noticed that they were doing about 30 percent of their business in Europe.

I knew Europe to be a very sophisticated, demanding market for fashionable shoes and clothing. I took a second look at my Timberland shoes and I realized that they were classically made and had the look of quality about them. The family that owned the company had a 40 percent stake in the business. Two years before Timberland went public, two brothers had inherited the company from their father, and one brother bought the other brother out for about $60 million. The company took out loans to purchase that brother's shares, and then they went public and used the proceeds of the initial public offering to pay back the loans.

Timberland had been in business for three generations, a fact I found a little romantic, since my family was also in the garment business. I didn't think I had learned anything working for my father for those four years, but I realized now that I had learned more than I'd thought. Back then, one of my responsibilities was to go around into retail stores and look at product. So I developed the ability to get comfortable walking around department stores and just looking at the shoes, the clothes, the product placement, and how any given retail store sold things.

So now I started to do the same thing with Timberland. I walked through a bunch of stores, saw how the shoes were displayed, liked what I saw, and made the decision to buy the stock.

Back then, Timberland stock sold for about $20 a share, and the company had a market capitalization of about $200 million, which, frankly, is minuscule in that industry. Nike was (and still is) the big dog in that field, and had done something no shoe company had ever done before: It had captured 25 percent of the worldwide market for shoes. Nike had almost singlehandedly caused the change in men's fashion from leather shoes to sneakers. It had created a market, captured the market, and were holding onto it for dear life. So who was this upstart Timberland to challenge Nike? Honestly, a nobody.

At the same time, I just felt *good* about the shoes and the boots Timberland made. As I said, I respected the quality and the classic look, and I was intrigued that it was marketed for outdoor use—which lent it a certain a mystique.

Now, 75 percent of the people who buy Nike shoes don't use them for sports. They just use them to look good or to walk around. Timberland, similarly, had a reputation for being an outdoor boot—even though the majority of people who bought Timberlands did not go mountain climbing. It just had the appeal of making you *think* about going outdoors. You look at a pair of Timberland boots and you think about getting outside. Do you actually go anywhere? Who cares?

I'll tell you another experience I had with Timberland that really attached me to the brand. One time I was in a Foot Locker store, just looking around, when I noticed that a woman was retuning a pair of Timberlands for credit. "What's wrong with the shoes?" the clerk asked.

"They're worn out," she explained, and she showed him that the bottoms of the shoes were indeed worn. It turned out that she had worn the shoes consistently for six months, so of course they were worn down. A lot of people do this—they wear out a product and then they go back and demand a refund.

To my surprise, the Foot Locker clerk told her that since Timberland had a liberal return policy, he would accept the shoes for full credit. I was impressed. It said a lot about the company that they were willing to give up a small amount of cash in exchange for a whole lot of good will. They had me, plain and simple.

The fastest-growing part of Timberland's market was in Europe, and the son of the owner had spent the last three years in Europe developing that market. It was remarkable and highly unusual for an American footwear company to be making those kinds of inroads in Europe back in 1993. Europeans never wanted to wear anything Americans made. Now, though, they were buying Nike and Timberland, and Calvin Klein underwear—but these were the only companies other than Levi's Jeans to capture a piece of the European market, which meant that Timberland was doing something right.

The capper came when I went into a high-end menswear boutique on Madison Avenue and overheard some Italians looking at Timberland boots and talking about how wonderful they were, how high quality they were, how beautiful they looked.

They were speaking Italian, and they couldn't stop raving about them—*Molto belle!*

And I thought to myself, "Italians marveling over an American shoe brand! Italians, who practically have a sense of footwear styling in their DNA, raving. As an aside, I also thought that since I had studied Romance languages at the university, "Maybe I can finally make a buck with my education."

That was enough for me: I went all in on Timberland. And in just nine months, the share price roared all the way from $20 to $80. And I told myself, "This is fabulous! Look at this! I'm a genius!"

I was happy, my clients were happy, everybody was happy. Then the company, under the son's leadership, got really aggressive trying to increase their sales from $200 million a year to $600 million. Unfortunately, they were too aggressive about the growth, and the stock fell all the way back to $20. They had overproduced, and they had to sell a lot of goods at closeout prices. They had done $400 million worth of sales the previous year and earned maybe $16 million in profit . . . but the next year they did $600 in million sales and profits were down.

Even though the stock fell back to earth, I remember being impressed that they hadn't actually lost money. I was still intrigued by them. At that time, a friend of mine in the business gave me a printout from a brokerage firm that said, in a nutshell, "Don't buy Timberland." The rationale was that even in the best of times, the company couldn't make a buck. It was discouraging. But I still believed that they soon would get the company right, and they would start making real money again. So I decided to give them another year or two before I sold.

Did everybody support me? Of course not! When the stock fell from $80 to $20, my brother, my lawyer, my accountant, my clients, my mother, and even my psychiatrist told me to get out! My psychiatrist! He actually told me that I had an obsession with the stock, and that it was insane for me to be so attached to it.

That really hurt! I stayed in Timberland *for another sixteen years*—and in that time it went from $20 all the way to $320, when the VF Corporation bought it out. How do you like that?

I was hardly an overnight success; it took a long time for the stock to even get back to $80, let alone to $320. I had put a hundred thousand dollars into it, and I reaped a million seventeen years later when I sold in 2010.

Do most investors have the patience to hang in there for so many years? Hardly. Do most investors have the steel to stand up to relatives, professionals, and even their psychiatrist? Of course not. But I stayed the course: I kept the stock and fired the psychiatrist. And that's story one of how I beat the market.

* * *

Anybody who says lightning never strikes twice needs to talk to me. I found another stock to obsess over in 2011 after the Timberland windfall of $1 million. It happened on a trip to London, where I somehow got to talking with a reporter about how happy I was to find ginger ale at my hotel. Back then there was nothing I loved more than ginger ale; it was by far my favorite beverage. Other people may like scotch and soda, or a cold beer, but give me a ginger ale on ice any day. (What can I say? I'm easy to please!)

So for whatever reason, the reporter and I got to talking about ginger ale, and she suggested that I buy something called the SodaStream machine, explaining that she had been interviewing the company for an article about homemade soda. I wasn't really that interested in homemade soda, however; I was perfectly happy to go buy a case of ginger ale at the store and drink it down, so that seemed to be the end of that.

A few months later, however, I saw that SodaStream had gone public. I thought, "That's the company we were talking about in London!" So I went and bought the stock—not a ton of it, but some. Then I went out and bought the product itself. By then, I had realized that my ginger ale habit wasn't healthful—I was consuming 130 calories a glass—so I'd started to drink sparkling water instead. And now with my SodaStream machine, I was able to make sparkling water for myself at a cost of twenty-five cents on the dollar compared to what I would have spent at the store, and there was no need to go back to the store to recycle the bottles.

So I said to myself, this company has a really good product and it fills a niche. The niche was essentially about convenience. If you bought two canisters of CO_2 you'd be set for a couple of months, and then you could return those to the store for credit when you got new canisters. The water was high quality compared even to San Pellegrino or Perrier, and you could control the level of carbonation. What's not to like? Ten times the convenience, a third of the cost of bottled sparkling water—this is a great product! So I started buying more of the stock for myself, and also for my clients.

Then suddenly the stock got hot—even Jim Cramer was pushing it on TV. He didn't really know anything about the company; all he knew was that it was going up. He tends to latch onto momentum, and the stock had gone from $20 a share to over $40. He actually had SodaStream come in and do a taste test on his show. None of the people who tried SodaStream cola on that show could distinguish it from Pepsi or Coca-Cola, and that demonstration had an effect on the stock. SodaStream went gangbusters, and began growing at 100 percent a year in the US market.

Then their US sales that had exploded came down quickly, because homemade flavored soda was a fad. Cramer panned the stock, citing a dispute with Target over placement in their stores. I thought this was ridiculous. The company's management was just as good when the stock was going down as it had been when the stock was going up. But those financial news networks, and especially Cramer's show, are not news shows. They're more like reality TV, designed just to get you excited.

As an experiment, I gave SodaStream machines to ten different people I knew as gifts. I wasn't being generous; it was marketing curiosity. I wanted to see who liked it and who didn't. The ones who used it for seltzer loved it, but the ones who only used it for flavored soda soon stopped using it. So I thought, "The play with this is going to be sparkling water."

Now, at around this time everyone suddenly started noticing that soda contained a whole lot of empty calories. So I thought to myself, "If I hang in there with SodaStream, it's going to become attractive to one of the big cola companies." Another small company, Green Mountain Coffee Roasters, had recently attracted a billion-dollar investment from Coca-Cola. I realized these soda companies were looking at declining sales as people became more health-conscious, and they had to find other, healthier products to get into.

Like seltzer. Like SodaStream.

And sure enough, SodaStream got a deal with Pepsi, and the stock made a fortune for all of its investors, my clients and me among them. I made 4.8 times the $1 million initial investment in 2011 when SodaStream went from 30 to 144 in 2018.

So I hear you saying, "Gene, if you beat the market twice, why can't you do it a third time? And why aren't you recommending to readers that they try to do the same thing?"

It's a fair question. I'm really not big on the "do as I say, not as I do" mentality when it comes to raising children or investing in the market. But the reality is that I got incredibly lucky . . . twice.

Part of it was that I had the strategic patience to hang in there with these companies for years, as both took torturous paths to the top. I could've cut my losses at any point along the way, as everybody on planet earth was telling me to do (even the people at my brokerage house—but more about that later). But I had done my homework, so I stayed with those stocks and got lucky.

That $100,000 investment in Timberland in 1993 became $4.8 million through investing the $1 million profit from Timberland into SodaStream in 2010–11. That's forty-eight times my initial investment in twenty-five years, about a 17 percent compounded return—the most important word being "compounded."

I'm not trying to convince you, as Peter Lynch did in *Beating the Street*, that anybody can do what I did. Most people don't put anywhere near the time into individual stocks that I did. As I've said, I put more than two thousand hours of research into each of those companies. Compare that with the lazy man's way to "success"—you hear Jim Cramer touting a stock, you run to your laptop, and you buy a few hundred shares. If it doesn't pan out in a few weeks, you're out of the stock and onto something else. That's the mentality of most "investors" (and I use the term guardedly in this context). That's not investing; it's betting on the Giants to cover the spread—and we all know how *that* typically turns out.

If you analyze these stories, you will see certain common threads. In both cases I just stumbled onto the stock, in one case by buying a pair of shoes and in another case through a random conversation with a British reporter. There's no rhyme or reason to those things, so it's not as if I can teach you to replicate those moments. Yes, you can look around at things that you think are valuable and could become successful stocks—but will you have the time to do the kind of homework and analysis necessary to determine whether they are worthy candidates for your hard-earned investment dollars? Unless you're in the industry, I tend to doubt it. Most people are simply too busy with their lives to do that kind of homework. And unless you are obsessed with the market, as I was from age eleven, you won't even want to do all that work. Unless you just eat, sleep, and breathe this stuff, it's boring.

Even if you find a company worthy of your investment dollars, and you manage to pour all the necessary time into analysis of the fundamentals of the company—its management, its sales history, its products, how it's marketed, how it's sold, what the future holds—will you still have the patience to sit there and hang on? If it goes up a bunch, will you sell it, happy to take a profit but unwilling to ride the elevator all the way to the top? Or if it starts to go down, will you lose your nerve and possibly even take a loss on the whole thing?

These are the questions you've got to ask yourself if you're seriously going to undertake investing in individual stocks. I can tell you that since Timberland and SodaStream, I have searched and searched for a third stock to get behind in the same manner, and I'm sad to report that I have not found one. I know how to hunt unicorns—I found two—but I'm telling you that I cannot find a third. Do you think you're going to be a better unicorn hunter than I am? Do you think you're going to be a better unicorn hunter than the entire stock market?

The forces arrayed against any individual investor are so massive that truly only a masochist or a delusional individual would think that he or she could crack the code. Remember that before I found the first of those two stocks, I had worked for fifteen years as a broker, and in that whole time I had never beaten the market. Never!

My success stories must be seen in the context of fifteen years of failure to beat the market, and my failure to find a third stock after SodaStream got bought out. So the moral of the story is, don't try this at home. These are sexy stories; I understand. These are stories I could take to the cocktail party or the golf course, and I could use them to drive a lot of business. But I'm past all that: I don't need the business. I'm not looking for new clients. All I'm looking to do is educate people—you, specifically—about what works and what doesn't work in the market.

Stop trying to hunt unicorns. Instead, do what works. And in the next chapter, I'm going to show you it works time after time after time. It may not be sexy, and it may not be a great story to tell at the club, but it's going to generate the kind of wealth that you're hoping for.

CHAPTER 3

If You Can't Beat the Market, Buy the Market

The funny thing about trying to make money in the stock market is that most people expect two things from their investments. The first is that they make a lot of money, preferably really quickly, and the second is that there's a really sexy story about how they're making money that they can tell the next time they go to the cocktail party or the locker room at the golf club.

I say pick one.

You can either invest in an asset class that is going to take good care of you and your money, or you can have a great story to tell. But you can't have both.

That's because the investment strategy I'm going to share with you in this chapter is so simple that it's going to sound boring to all of your stock-tip-loving, Jim Cramer–watching, financial news–addicted chums at the cocktail party, at the golf club, or at the marina.

Of course, it's plenty sexy to have an investment that is all but guaranteed to make you real money over the long haul. So if you can set aside that deep-rooted need that so many investors have, the desire for the really cool story that gets you nods of approbation wherever you and your friends gather, then listen up. Because I'm going to change your financial life.

You've already heard of SPY, the Russell 2000, and QQQ. You just may not realize how effective they are for 99.9 percent of investors—the ones whose last names aren't Buffett or Lynch.

These three entities are known as exchange-traded funds (ETFs). They are essentially a basket of stocks that allow you to purchase not one or two or three individual stocks or high-fee funds from your financial advisor. Instead, they allow you to buy the entire market all at once.

Spydrs are a basket containing the five hundred biggest "large cap" stocks that are included in the S&P 500. These include Coty Inc., QUALCOMM, and Xerox.

The QQQ is a basket containing the top hundred stocks on the Nasdaq, which is where technology stocks are traded. These include Apple, Microsoft, Alphabet/Google, and a host of other companies whose names you may or may not recognize.

The Russell 2000 is a basket of small cap stocks—the two thousand largest "small cap" companies that trade on the markets today.

Why are these funds called exchange-traded funds? Simply put, because they are bought and sold on stock exchanges the same way individual stocks are bought and sold. Mutual funds, by contrast, only trade once a day, at the end of the day. ETFs go up and down over the course of the day, depending on how the stocks contained in those funds are doing.

So if you invest in Spydrs, you are buying the S&P 500, the largest stocks on the market. If you're buying QQQ, you're buying the hundred biggest Nasdaq stocks. And if you're buying the Russell 2000, you're buying the two thousand biggest small cap stocks.

It's that simple.

One of the themes of this book is that it's impossible for any human being to intelligently and completely track more than a few stocks. So we're not looking to buy advice on which stocks will go up or down. What we are doing is making a bet that history, in a broad sense, will repeat itself. Over most ten-year periods the stock market has been up. So it's extremely likely, short of World War III, that ten years from now the market will be up. Twenty years from now, the market will be up even more. Thirty years from now, the market will be up. And so on, all the way out to the end of your investment horizon. You are buying the entire market for big companies, small companies, or tech companies. If the market goes up, your investment goes up. Since inevitably the market goes up, it is all but inevitable that your investment into one of these three exchange-traded funds will go up.

Is it sexy? Is it fun? Is it exciting? Does it give you a great story to tell your buddies? No, it will do none of the above for you. Instead, all it will do is make you more money.

And isn't that the only sensible reason for going into the stock market? To make more money?

You want to pay somebody to go to your daughter's wedding, I'm not going to stop you. You want to pay to have someone to call on the phone when the market goes down and you get a little scared? Knock yourself out. You want to watch Jim Cramer and his ilk and get into this stock and out of that stock and out of that stock until you can't even think straight? I'm not coming over to your house and taking away your laptop or whatever device you use for trading. But you've got to choose between having an investment that is about as sure a thing as exists on God's green earth and having a really cool story to tell your buddies. Pick one.

So how do you buy ETFs? The same way you buy individual stocks. Call your broker or go to their website. Type in SPY for Spydrs, QQQ for the Nasdaq, or IWM for the small cap stocks, or just buy the very low-cost Vanguard S&P Index Fund—the cost is under one-tenth of 1 percent annually. Figure out how much money you want to put into it, and you're done. Now go about the rest of your business, because you've just handled your investment responsibilities for the next fifty years.

I hear you asking, "Could it really be that simple? Investing in stocks is complicated. That's why we have advisors!"

No. We have advisors because advisors have convinced us that investing is complicated. At heart, it's simple. Over time, the market always goes up. So buy the market. Don't pay people 1 percent if, ninety-four out of a hundred times, they are not going to do as well as you, sitting pretty with your ETF or index fund. You bought the market. They can't keep up with the market. You win.

You get to keep your 1 percent, by the way. And that adds up considerably over a lifetime. Again, if you really want to enrich your financial advisor at your own expense, I'm certainly not going to get in your way. I may question your sanity, but I'll never tell you that because I don't want to hurt your feelings.

Now I hear you asking, "But what if I want to pick stocks?" or "What if I want to let my broker pick stocks for me? After all, don't they have all that inside information that the regular person doesn't have access to?"

It may be worth taking a moment to remind you that the use of inside information when buying or selling securities is a crime. That's true whether it's an individual doing it for themselves or a broker or investment firm doing it on behalf of clients. So the question is not, what inside information do they have that I can tap into if I'm a client? The real question is, how would my broker and I look in jumpsuits and bath slippers if we were caught, arrested, and convicted for using inside information?

Let's get real. They don't have any inside information. They want you to *think* they do. Their websites hint at all sorts of dark secrets of the marketplace that they know about and can only share with their clients. But if they really had access to any kind of special information, why would 94 percent of them trail the market over any meaningful period of time?

Some readers may be old enough to remember that back in the 1980s, the *Wall Street Journal* had a fun competition every month in their financial section. They would invite stockbrokers to pick a couple of stocks, and then the reporters would throw darts at a dartboard. Then they would see who came out ahead over a six-month period. Guess what? More often than not, the darts won. I figured that they had to stop running the feature because they ran out of advisors who were comfortable getting beaten by darts.

I'll tell you about an even bigger bet: A hedge fund guy put up a million dollars of his own cash against a million dollars of Warren Buffett's money that he could outperform the S&P Index over a ten-year period.

The hedge fund guy lost. He had to pay Buffett the million dollars.

Of course, for a hedge fund guy, a million dollars is a rounding error, the amount of money that falls out of his pocket and goes into the couch cushions whenever he stands up. And on top of that, it was good publicity for the guy. So for him, losing a million dollars was no big deal, and it got his name in the paper. What's not to like?

For people like you and me, however, losing any amount of money is serious business. Failing to maximize on an investment strategy is almost as bad as outright losses. That money should stay in your pocket, not go into the pocket of your investment advisor.

So now you're probably asking, "Why doesn't my broker put me into an ETF or index fund if they're such a great investment?"

There are a lot of reasons. The first one is that ETFs are no secret. Type the letters into Google and you'll find plenty of websites explaining exactly what ETFs are, what they do, how successful they are, and how to buy them. So there's every possibility that if your broker said to you, "I'm going to put you in an ETF," you might end up saying, "An ETF? I could've done that by myself! What do I need you for?"

Those six words, "What do I need you for," are the precise words that no broker ever wants to hear. They want to hear, "Wow, great job! You're so smart!" not "What do I need you for?"

The second reason why brokers seldom put their clients' investable assets into an ETF is that firms make money when they buy and sell. Why would you ever want to sell an ETF? It's the best possible investment for the long haul.

One of my friends told me, "I just bought a stock that I'm planning to hold for five years. The only problem is that I check it every hour or two." Most people simply don't have the strategic patience to hold onto a stock for the length of time that Warren Buffett prescribes—which is forever. People want action. They are addicted to action. They want to see movement, even if it doesn't make them money. They want to think that their advisor is doing something for them.

Well, if he isn't putting you into an ETF, or if he's selling an ETF just because it went up a little bit, he's not exactly doing you a favor. Firms cannot make money on a "buy and hold forever" strategy. But again, you have to ask, for whom are you trying to make money? You, or your broker and his or her firm?

In other words, whom are you trying to impress with all your cool stock tips? Your buddies at the club? Or yourself, your spouse, and your children and grandchildren when you're able to provide financial security for them, pay for college, take care of retirement expenses, and leave a meaningful amount of money behind. Again, pick one.

There's another reason why financial advisors are not overly interested in ETFs. It's because typically, brokerage houses only want to sell products—funds or other investment opportunities—that were created by the company itself.

It used to be that they weren't even permitted to sell something "outside of the family" to their clients. In other words, a Morgan Stanley stockbroker was completely unable to sell you a Vanguard fund or a Fidelity fund. They would either tell you that they couldn't buy it for you or they might tell you it wasn't in your best interests, depending on how honest they were.

Today, the rules have changed, and your broker might be able to sell you funds created elsewhere. The problem is that the commissions are lower, both for the individual broker and for the firm. So if your broker is continually putting his clients into investments that net low fees for the firm, at some point, he is going to get the dreaded call, email, or visit from his manager asking what's going on.

One of the themes of this book is that the investment firms exist primarily to make money for themselves and only secondarily to make money for you. Indeed, if they haven't done poorly, then both you and they think they had a pretty good day.

But that's not good enough for you, is it?

The challenge in presenting this investment approach is that in many ways, I'm taking away your fun. Investing can be addictive. You've got all the highs and lows of going to Vegas, betting the under in a game with your favorite football team, skydiving, bungee jumping, or any other life experience that involves risk. All I'm saying is that you've been unconsciously risking way too much money for way too long. If you are willing to give up the psychological thrill of investments that you get into and out of, then buy an ETF. You'll sleep better at night.

If you want to take a small amount of your money—say, 5 percent—and throw it at individual stocks for entertainment value, then knock yourself out if you can afford to do so. Again, I'm not coming over to your house to keep you from doing what you want to do.

All I'm saying is that people who buy individual stocks typically trail the market, often by a lot. People who keep their money with investment advisors trail the market 94 percent of the time over the long haul. And people who invest with fraudsters like Madoff or Ponzi can lose everything.

So come on over to the smart side of the street. Maybe it's a little boring over here, but there's never anything boring about opening up the envelope with your statement in it and seeing that, over the long haul, all you've done is make money—and lots of it.

It's not sexy, but it gets you there. I hope you'll agree with me by now that ETFs and index funds are the way to go.

CHAPTER 4

The Problem with Modern Portfolio Theory

Performance doesn't matter.
**—Frank Novello, branch manager,
NYC Morgan Stanley Office**

A guy named Harry Markowitz invented what's called Modern Portfolio Theory, which practically every financial advisor in the world—probably including yours—buys into. He presented his theory in a paper called "Portfolio Selection," which was published in March of 1952 by the *Journal of Finance*. Every brokerage house ought to be paying him a commission, because Modern Portfolio Theory, or MPT, has become the leading standard for modern advisors and brokerage firms. But here's what all those advisors and brokerage firms won't tell you: MPT could be losing you money.

Let me explain.

Modern Portfolio Theory isn't bad. It's just not particularly good. MPT lowers risk and increases diversification. But while your advisors are protecting you from potential losses, they're also protecting you from extraordinary gains.

And they're charging you for that privilege.

Based on information, the advisors will then use complex mathematical formulas—or computer programs provided by the investment firms, or just simply a gut feeling about the market—to construct a portfolio just for you. That portfolio will likely consist of fifty to one hundred stocks, which may or may not include some from every index.

The goal of these portfolios is to have what's called balance. The idea is that you are spreading your bets over a variety of investment types, so that you have multiple chances to be successful. At the same time, if you are overly exposed to one particular asset class, let's say large caps, and they were to take a tumble relative to the rest of the market, you would not be overly invested in that group. As a result, your portfolio would not suffer as much.

But to maintain that balance, a manager will often sell a gain too early. This is the single biggest mistake that an investor will ever make: selling their winners too early.

Let's imagine for a moment that we were at the roulette table at a casino. You can put the money on red or black; one through eighteen or nineteen through thirty-six; the lower third, the middle third, or the top third; or on individual numbers. How can you make the most money? By making one bet and pushing all your chips onto that one section of the felt table for the croupier to note.

At a roulette table, of course, it's pure gambling, and the house has a strong advantage. Ever notice those numbers zero and double zero? Statistically, they will come up often enough to ensure that all bets lose. So when you're in a casino playing roulette, good luck. The odds are always against you.

What about MPT? Again, you're making a wide series of bets, putting money down on all sorts of different propositions: Small caps. Medium caps. Large caps. Foreign stocks. Service stocks. Tech stocks. Auto stocks. And so on and so forth, depending on your perceived risk tolerance. The wheel spins . . . and chances are, most of your bets are losers.

Maybe not losers in the sense that they actually lose you money, but in the sense that they don't keep up with the market. As I've said repeatedly throughout this book, you would've been much better off if you'd put all your money in an ETF or an index fund that mirrors the market. Why?

Because by having professional management, you put a ceiling on how much money you can make.

As I said earlier, we're looking at those stocks not as businesses or groups of businesses, but as simply pieces of paper.

We're hoping that some of those pieces of paper will go up in value, and we're hoping that the ones that go down don't drop too far. We're looking at a bet on an investment, rather than ownership of individual companies.

There are individual investors who have enormous insight into any given company. But they can't possibly know two hundred companies, as our friend Jim Cramer claims to. They cannot know every stock on the market, regardless of what they read on the Bloomberg terminals in their offices. So you are making bets not against the MGM Grand or the Bellagio, but against the entire marketplace—which knows better. The stock market has sophisticated people in it, and you're always making a bet with or against them.

Of course, your friendly investment advisor will never tell you that. It's the last thing he or she wants to think about. You know why they're selling you MPT?

Well, it does benefit you. It benefits you through diversification and through risk management. But mostly, it protects them.

MPT is a way to protect against volatility, and volatility goes both ways. It won't lose you a lot of money and it won't gain you a lot of money either. And that keeps clients happy.

If their calculations are right, then they will never lose more money for you than you say you can stand losing. If you tell them that you are comfortable with a lot of risk, then they can lose you a lot of money and then point back to that conversation and say, "But you said you were OK with big risk!"

If, on the other hand, you indicated that your risk tolerance was low, they could lose you a little money, and you have no recourse. "You told us that you could tolerate a small amount of risk. Unfortunately, the worst happened, and your portfolio is down. But our decisions were based on what *you*, the investor, told us you wanted, so don't blame us."

The investment house can say and do pretty much anything it wants in accordance with your risk tolerance profile, because it can claim that any loss or failure to keep up with the market is a function of the risk tolerance you put down in writing. And it can cut any potential gains short, with the excuse of rebalancing. It is essentially absolved from having to create better returns for you than if MPT had never been invented.

MPT demands diversity and diversity is great. But you can get that practically for free by buying an index fund or an ETF—and an index fund isn't going to sell off its best-performing stocks.

Let's look at what happens if one sector becomes successful. Let's say that one of your "bets" is on the tech sector. And let's say that for whatever reason, tech goes wild. Google, Facebook, Apple, Microsoft—they all shoot up. After all, the fundamentals that drove tech forward this week are likely to keep it moving forward the following week, and maybe for months or years to come. It's a great bet!

So what does your broker do? Does he take money from the other sectors—small cap, autos, foreign, whatever—sell those off and stick them into tech so that you can benefit even more abundantly from this winning bet?

Amazingly, he will do the opposite. *He will sell off the tech and put it back into the other categories that are currently just treading water or even losing money.*

You heard me right—when a sector in a portfolio built on MPT starts to surge, your friendly financial advisor will sell off the holdings in that sector, in order to bring the portfolio back into "balance."

Financial advisors and financial services firms love balanced portfolios. Why? Because it reduces the risk they carry. The magic word for them is *exposure*. They want to avoid exposure like the plague. Exposure means they have all of your money (and everyone else's money) in a particular stock or sector. Let's say that stock or sector tumbles. Now the firm is out tons of money, all the portfolios in the firm are down, and an army of unhappy clients will call up and say, "What happened? You used to be so smart! I've had enough—and I'm leaving! Sell everything and send me a check."

That's exposure. That's a nightmare for financial services firms.

When clients are unhappy, they don't just leave. Sometimes they sue. The magic word in those lawsuits is *suitability*, meaning they are claiming that the investment the firm put them into was not suitable for their net worth, their level of income, their risk tolerance, and so on. It's a real hassle to fight suitability lawsuits. It's expensive, it's unpleasant, and it affects the firm's image, as well as the image of the individual financial advisor.

So the most important thing in the world for them is to prevent the possibility of waves of unhappy clients. How do they do that? By avoiding exposure to one particular stock or asset class. When you avoid that kind of exposure, you limit exposure to suitability lawsuits, unhappy clients, bad headlines, and so on.

So when the advisor sells off those beautiful, high-flying stocks in your portfolio, whom is he helping? You? Hardly! The goal is to cut losses short, and profits too. You want to let that bet ride a little longer and continue to capture the upside. But they don't want that. They don't understand that it's in your best interest to keep those fabulous companies in your portfolio. They want to get rid of them, because they want balance more than they want you to make more money.

Does this sound like a harsh indictment of the entire financial services sector? I suppose it does. But in a situation like this, who wins? As the expression goes, follow the money.

And in this case, the money goes from your pocket to theirs, because you are no longer in the game to enjoy the benefits of the rise of the stocks in that sector—while they are no longer at risk for unhappy clients and suitability lawsuits due to overexposure in any given sector or stock.

So if you're an investor, MPT sounds great. What could go wrong? My broker is trying to get to know me and my risk tolerance. But the reality is that *everybody* hates risk. Everybody hates losing.

So people will make statements about themselves and their supposed risk tolerance that aren't even grounded in reality!

"How much risk can you handle?" the advisor asks.

"Lots and lots," the client says firmly.

"Great," says the advisor. "Sign here."

The client signs with a great big flourish. He's practically writing in all capital letters, I LOVE RISK! But investors don't love risk. They love making money. And whether you claim that you have a high tolerance for risk or a low tolerance, the reality is that with MPT, you are making a bet against your own greater interest as an investor. You're hedging your bets. Instead of doing homework, or having someone do homework for you on the real merits of each individual stock within that portfolio, you are trusting your financial future to a computer that benefits the house every time, because the computers at the Morgan Stanleys and Raymond Jameses of the world will simply not permit unbalanced portfolios.

I experienced this personally when I was at Morgan Stanley. As you know by now, I was in love with SodaStream. The more it went up, the more unbalanced my portfolio and my clients' portfolios became. Morgan Stanley was getting exposed!

So guess what happened? Sure enough, I got a knock on the door from my manager. "You're overexposed. It's not OK. The computer won't permit it."

"But I'm making money for the clients," I protested.

"We don't care," the manager said. "Cut it out. You've got to sell those shares in SodaStream. The computer will not allow us to have that sort of imbalance, that sort of exposure."

I actually had to send letters to all my clients explaining that they were overexposed to SodaStream in their portfolios, and they had to sign a letter and send it back to me saying that they were OK with that. And even those letters weren't enough. The computer—and the company—would not allow me to keep those stocks in their Morgan Stanley investment accounts. I actually had to find a different mechanism for holding onto those shares so I would not miss the continued upside growth, and that's exactly what I did.

Why did I do all that? Because I had invested two thousand hours of my time learning all about SodaStream, understanding the market, giving away machines to friends, gauging their reactions, and coming away with a conviction that this was a company to stay in for the long haul. But Morgan Stanley didn't care about any of that.

Now, this isn't a rap on Morgan Stanley in particular. They were just doing what any of the large brokerage houses would've done. If I had been at Merrill Lynch, it would've been the same way. All that matters is what the computer says, because the computer is protecting the house, not the individual investor. It goes back to the roulette table, where you've got the zero and the double zero. Whom do those numbers protect? That's right. The house. Having a zero and double zero on the roulette wheel reduces the casino's exposure to loss, the same way that the rebalancing requirement in an MPT portfolio protects the brokerage house.

But it's crazy to sell winners!

Look, if you want to be protected from making more money, then ignore everything I'm saying. But if what I'm saying makes sense, then ask yourself why you have a portfolio that is going to cut the legs out from any successful investment that you happen to make. Your financial advisor is protecting himself and you from losses by limiting your upside. That's what they do.

It all comes back to the question of whether you are looking at investments and stocks as pieces of paper or as the ownership of companies that consist of management teams, employees, products, and services. If they're pieces of paper to you, then you might as well be at the casino. I don't know the exact figures on people who don't beat the house at casinos, but I'm sure it's not too far from the 94 percent of investment advisors who fail to beat the market. If you want to be one of those people, I don't even know why you're reading my book. But if you're open to the idea that since you can't beat the market, you may as well buy the market, then you and I have something to talk about.

Is MPT for losers? That's a pretty harsh way to look at things. It's not for losers. It's just not the way to get maximum possible returns. MPT puts too low a ceiling on winners, all in the name of protecting the interests of the financial services firm.

It's reassuring to get a call from your advisor and be told that he has rebalanced your portfolio, because it makes you feel as though your advisor is looking out for your best interests. And he is. But he's also looking out for the best interests of the firm and himself, and those best interests may keep you from capturing the value you could.

Harry Markowitz, may he rest in peace, has made a lot of money for individual advisors and their investment firms in the nearly seven decades since he first published that article. If only he had done as much for individual investors. But he hasn't, and if your portfolio is based on his ideas, it's time to rethink the whole thing.

Five Reasons Why Your Advisor Can't Beat the Market

If you look at the ads on TV, in newspapers or magazines, or online, you get the sense that every financial services firm has a magic touch when it comes to making money for their clients. Every ad says the same thing: We're up 15 percent over the last ten years, annualized return. Our international stocks were up 37 percent over the last eighteen months. Our small caps were up 42 percent over the last five years. You look at these ads and you conclude that these people are all geniuses! They all have the Midas touch!

This is why it's so compelling for most people to turn their money over to a financial advisor who, no doubt, will replicate those fabulous successes and make them fantastic amounts of money. All for that minuscule 1 percent. What could go wrong?

Actually, let's ask a different question. If, as we've seen, 94 percent of advisors don't beat the market over the long term, then how could every single ad for financial services firm depict gains that not only beat the market but crush it?

The simple answer is that the firms cherry-pick their results. If you are a big financial services company, you have your fingers in a lot of pies: small cap, large cap, international, commodities, bonds—you name it.

No matter how well or how poorly you have done for any given client, you can inevitably find numbers that indicate fantastic success over some period of time for something that you've done. You may have underperformed the market, and maybe very few of your clients have made as much money with you as they would have if they'd bought and held onto an unsexy ETF. But there are ways to slice and dice and cherry-pick the data to make the lowliest stock picker look like Warren Buffett.

Are the numbers in the ads true? Of course they are. But there's nothing to stop these firms from hiring smart people and locking them in a room with tons of data and telling them, "We aren't going to unlock the door until you find some statistics that make us look good."

These people want to see their loved ones again. Maybe they just want a change of clothes or a hot meal! So they are going to pound furiously on their laptops until they come up with numbers that make the firm look great. Maybe the investing in international stocks that the firm has done over a ten-year period has been a disaster, so they won't tell you that they've gotten great returns on their international stocks for the last ten years. But maybe the last eighteen months were pretty good, so there's one data point to cherry-pick and display proudly.

Maybe their luck with small caps over the last twenty years has been nothing to write home about. Ah, but take a look at small caps over the last four years and eight months! Up 23 percent! (The previous sixteen months? Don't ask.)

You get the point. You cannot look at the flashy numbers these investment advisors are displaying in those ads and say to yourself, "I bet they can get me those same returns." Chances are, they didn't get *anybody* those returns! These are strands of data pulled out of an overall web of information about the performance of the entire firm over a period of five, ten, or twenty years. How did they really do? You know the answer by now. Ninety-four percent of the time, they lagged the market. Can they legally claim the great results they are advertising? Absolutely! They aren't lying. They are being disingenuous, however, because they want you believe something that isn't true. They want you to believe that these cherry-picked numbers actually reflect real results that this firm has achieved for others—and more to the point, that they can accomplish for you.

In short, don't believe the hype. Don't believe those ads.

At the same time, highly intelligent people work in these companies analyzing stocks, making recommendations, and working directly with the clients. They live, eat, and breathe the market every day, just as I do. So why is there such a disconnect between their considerable abilities and their often disappointing outcomes?

In this chapter, I'd like to explore with you five reasons why portfolio managers consistently fail to outperform the market. My goal is to demystify the process by which advisors work and market themselves, in order to arm you with a healthy skepticism about their claims.

Reason Number 1:
Short-Term Thinking

As we've said earlier, there's a tendency on the part of investors and advisors alike to look at a share of stock as a piece of paper rather than a representation of a percentage of ownership of an actual company that hires people and makes things. The result is short-term thinking, because the only question that matters is, "How much is this piece of paper worth today?" If the stock shoots up, that piece of paper is worth more, and everybody's happy. If the stock price falls off a cliff, the piece of paper is worth much less, and it's a disaster, and people fire their brokers. "How could you have put me into this thing? What were you thinking?"

But let me ask you this: The stock price may have been gyrating . . . but what about the fundamentals of the company? Did the quality of the management team suddenly increase or decrease? Did the products suddenly get better or worse? Or is it possible that the company provides so much value, and that its fundamentals are so strong, that the roller-coaster ride the stock price is taking does not truly reflect the underlying value of the company?

This is exactly the philosophy I adhered to while weathering the turmoil in both Timberland and SodaStream. I held on until the real value was recognized by getting a higher cash offer from other players in the industry.

If a guy gets on TV and says, "This stock is a dog and you've got to get out," there's going to be a stampede of sellers. But does this in any way affect the underlying value of the company? Of course not! Warren Buffett says that the stock market could close for a ten-year period and it would not bother him in the least, because he knows that the companies he has bought have ongoing value that isn't measured accurately by the short-term thinking of the market.

Your broker is not immune to short-term thinking. In fact, it's where most of them live, almost all the time. As we will see, they are simply not incentivized to think about the long term—for the stock, for you, or for anyone but themselves. And as we've discussed, even people who make rational, intelligent decisions about buying stock because they recognize the value in a particular company are still not immune to fear. People get scared, and they make investment decisions based on emotion rather than reason.

Ben Graham, the father of Value Investing, used to say that the stock market is like a voting machine: People vote based on how they feel. But just as in an election, sometimes people vote against their best interests without even realizing it. Short-term thinking—yours, the market's, and your advisor's—keeps you from enjoying the long-term potential that a well-managed company offers . . . and that is the atmosphere in which most advisors (and most of their clients!) operate. That's the first reason why advisors tend to underperform the market.

Reason Number 2:
They Have to Invest in Too Many Companies

As we've seen, investment firms consider it essential to minimize their exposure to any one stock, lest it tank and take down everybody's portfolio with it. As a result, financial advisors have to be knowledgeable about the hundreds of stocks they are managing in their portfolios.

I am here to tell you that it is absolutely impossible for any human being to do this well. I put two thousand hours each into Timberland and SodaStream: That's a full year's worth of work on each company. Unless your advisor is planning to live for two hundred years, how exactly is he or she going to spend all the necessary time to get to know any particular investment? Instead, they operate on limited information, and based on that limited information, they make bets with your financial future.

Your advisor may have as many as 250 different companies or investments in the portfolios they manage. Let me ask you this: Do you know any heart surgeons who perform 250 different types of operations? Would you trust one who did? Granted, your money isn't your life, but it's pretty close. Why are you expecting that one human being can do the kind of work necessary to keep track of all those companies, to really understand their management teams, their products, and their marketing strategies? On its face, the idea is absurd. And yet, this is how the market works.

This is the second reason why advisors seldom beat the market—they're trying to keep tabs on far more companies than they could possibly understand.

Reason Number 3:
They Get Paid to Keep Close
to the Market, Not to Beat It

Everybody acts in their own perceived economic self-interest. That's human nature. Your advisor knows that his bonus system will provide him with a seven-figure check if he simply sticks close to the market—he doesn't have the beat the market to get that bonus. But if he makes some big bets that fail to pay off, and he lags the market by a significant degree, he loses his bonus. Would you want to do that if you were in his shoes? Probably not!

So the tendency is to play it safe, to go for that big basket of stocks that may not go up by much, but probably won't go down by a ton. During the 2007–2008 downturn, if the market was down 60 percent and your advisor only lost you 45 percent, you thought he was a genius! Only on Wall Street can a person be considered a hero for losing a significant portion of a client's net worth.

That's the third reason why advisors lag the market—it's not in their economic self-interest to rock the boat, try to help you beat the market, and potentially lose their bonuses.

Reason Number 4:
Grabbing Quick Returns to Make Up
for the Dogs in a Portfolio

Let's say you have a portfolio of 250 stocks. Most won't move up or down very much, but some will do badly. If you had studied those companies, you might've seen that coming. But since the model doesn't give you time to get to know all of them, you're going to have some big losses on your accounts.

So what do you do to make up for that? You take a look at what stocks are going up, and you sell them so that you can lock in some gains to offset the losses you took. The returns may look pretty good, but you cut off at the knees the potential for real success you might have had with those winners. What good is getting a five-point gain on a stock, if, within two years, it's up fifty points? You don't think about it, because once you sell the stock, you stop looking at it. So you're not even going to realize how much money you left on the table, all because your advisor sold a winner to disguise the losses created by companies that lost a bunch of money.

That's the fourth reason why advisors seldom beat the market—your advisor has to sell the winners to compensate for the losers, and he has to rebalance the portfolio.

Reason Number 5:
The Computer Always Says No

I told you that when my clients had a lot of SodaStream in their accounts, the computer at Morgan Stanley went haywire. I got letters and I got visits: You've got to get out of this stock. The firm is overexposed. Your clients are overexposed.

You could say that fear is programed into the computers at the investment houses. Computer programs are far more concerned about the overall risk the firm faces if a stock tanks than about your ability to make money if the stock continues to rise. It's just not worth the hassle for advisors to fight the system. It doesn't make them look good around the office. They're considered the problem children. So the natural thing is to just go with the flow and sacrifice the rewards you could've gotten for your clients . . . because the computer won't let you.

* * *

So you might say, if 94 percent of advisors keep trailing the market, how can these companies make any money? The short answer is that they make their money on your cash. It may be more accurate to consider these financial services companies as banks rather than investment houses: They're taking the cash that you don't have invested at any particular moment, paying you a tiny amount of interest, and then lending it out at market rates. The firms literally make billions of dollars doing this. Your uninvested cash is their house in the Hamptons, their retirement, their grandchildren's college education. It all adds up. Even in an environment of no-fee stock trading, they're still making an incredible fortune, simply taking the money you have in cash, turning around, and investing it.

The short, sorry truth is that financial services firms won't beat the market on your behalf, but with your spare cash, and the spare cash of millions of other clients, they're making so much money that whether they succeed or fail for you just doesn't matter.

For this you're going to pay 1 percent a year forever? Here's hoping you don't.

CHAPTER 6

Day Trading, Commodities, and Investing Internationally: Three Losing Strategies

There are so many ways to underperform the market that you could fill a whole library with them. In this chapter, I'd like to share with you my thoughts on three approaches to investing that just don't work: day trading; commodities, including gold; and investing internationally.

Not all of these strategies lose money, but typically when they do go up, they don't generate the same level of return that you get when buying the market. Each is attractive for different reasons, but none of them lives up to the hype. So let's take a look at each of them, and you can determine for yourself whether any of them make sense. I'm sure you can already guess how I feel about each of them.

Let's start with day trading. It's impossible to make real money day trading. I'm being blunt because I want to disabuse you quickly of the notion that you can sit there at your computer all day long, or even spend a little time in the morning and a little time at night, and make tons of trades and somehow expect that you're going to come out way ahead.

I won't say that you *can't* make money in day trading; in a rising market, you will latch on, at least half the time, to stocks that are going up. The problem is that when you add in all the costs—fees, taxes, and your valuable time—there's simply no way that you will beat the market. Yes, if you're day trading religiously every business day for thirty years, you may well end up with more capital than you started with. But you have to measure that against the index. Your return will almost certainly be vastly below what you would have gotten with a buy-and-hold strategy or a buy-the-index strategy. You're simply giving up the possibility of an excellent wealth creation vehicle that involves much less expense and much less work.

Day Trading

Let's talk about what day trading really means. Each day, a day trader looks at what's going on in the market and makes a series of bets—I mean *investments*—on a number of stocks. The idea is to close out all of the trades by the end of the day, so you are not keeping anything long term. (By "long term," in this case, I mean tomorrow.) The strategy is very Jim Cramer–like. You are looking for signals that certain stocks have positive momentum, and you want to ride that momentum over the course of the day—hence the term *day trading*. You can put in orders to sell the stock if it goes up a certain amount, so you lock in a profit. You can also put in an order to sell if it drops to a certain level, so as to limit your losses.

Some day traders sit at their computers twelve hours a day, trading multiple stocks on multiple markets in multiple time zones. Others put some time into their day trading habit first thing in the morning, place their orders, and go off to work. I'm not sure how you can get a day's worth of work done without the distraction of wondering how your stocks are doing, or worse, checking them every fifteen minutes. That's a discipline that you're going to have to master if you're going to have a chance at succeeding at day trading *and* keep your day job. But that's basically how it works.

How do you know which stocks to buy? There are plenty of services that charge good money to encourage day traders to buy certain stocks. The people who really make money in day trading are the ones who sell information to day traders, not the day traders themselves! In fact, if you're looking for a good business model, you're better off touting stocks for a fee than trying to buy stocks and make money. It's a little like horse racing. The people who publish the *Daily Racing Form* make lots of money, while the bettors who study the information on each horse in each race—working with systems, deep levels of analysis, and hunches—inevitably lose. But at least they're having fun at the track with the excitement of watching the horses run. What can I say? To each his own.

Can you actually make money day trading? As I said, sure, if you are extremely good at it or if you are simply day trading in a bull market. I mean, even a broken clock is right twice a day, so why not some stock picks in a rising market? The problem is that, once again, you are looking at stocks as pieces of paper, or in this case the digital equivalent, instead of remembering that they are actual companies with actual management, actual products and services, and actual customers. You could pick out a stock based on its momentum over the last few days only to be blindsided by some news about the actual company that the shares of stock represent.

I know—who invited real information about real companies to the party? We're just trying to make a little money over here, right? But although day traders look at stocks as "investments," or the digital equivalent of pieces of paper, there are still real companies here doing real things in the real world. It's easy for day traders to ignore that basic reality.

Let's say that you actually make some money on your investments on any given day. You're going to pay short-term capital gains tax on the money you made. That's 35 percent. On the other hand, if you buy and hold and eventually sell, you are paying long-term capital gains rates—just 20 percent. There's a huge difference between paying 20 percent and paying 35 percent on the money you make. Do you really want to give up more than a third of your earnings to the government? Remember that they're not going to give you any money back on your losses! When you lose money, you are on your own, but when you make money, Uncle Sam has his hand in your pocket. When you win on a horse race, the track only takes 16 percent of your money. Yet one more reason to go to the races instead of trying day trading!

Why do you pay a much stiffer tax rate on day trading? One of the purposes of the tax code is to influence behavior. For example, there's a mortgage deduction that was created because the government made a policy decision to encourage people to own their own homes: People take better care of what they own than what they rent. Home ownership creates stability in communities. It also keeps people tied to their jobs, so it creates stability in society. That's an example of a policy decision reflected by the tax code.

Discouraging speculation by placing a high tax on short-term gains is another policy decision that Congress made years ago. A buy-and-hold strategy benefits from tax policy that discourages people from pure speculation. I'm not necessarily saying that Congress knows better than you what to do with your money. I am saying that they made a decision to reach in your pocket every time you speculate and make money, because that's not what they want people to do. If you're willing to pay that extra tax, then have a nice time day trading. But if you'd rather pay less tax, then you have to question whether the strategy of day trading makes sense for you.

The money that sits in your brokerage account overnight while you are not trading is going to make you minimal interest, if any, compared to what you could get in a money market fund. That's another hidden cost of day trading. Is it worth it? That's up to you.

Day traders are basically gamblers. They're saying, "I'm willing to lose up to 3 percent on an investment because I could make as much as 10 percent." It sounds great in theory, but when the rubber hits the road, it's really a lousy way to invest. It's extremely time-consuming: You have to spend time studying the market, seeing which stocks appear to have momentum; make the trades; and then see how things worked out at the end of the day. While you're busy doing this, the people who have their money in a buy-and-hold strategy, especially with ETFs and index funds, are enjoying life untethered to their computer screens. They're having meals with their families. They're playing with their kids. They're going to the gym or the movies, or watching something on Netflix. They're doing all the things that you cannot do, and at the same time, they're making more money than you are, because very few day traders ever create returns that approach the overall market index return.

Most day traders are hoping that some sort of good news comes out while their investment is live—the company announces a big deal, or they get FDA approval for a new drug, etc. To me, hope is not a good investment strategy.

When you think about it, it's often not even news about a company that gets people interested in that company. Instead, it's news that creates movement in the stock price that excites day traders. The actual news doesn't create the movement; it's the reaction of the market to that news. If that's your idea of a good time, then knock yourself out. Otherwise, what's the point?

And not all news is good news: Companies can report lower earnings. There could be a huge lawsuit. Tariffs or other international events can quickly push a stock price much lower. Are you really sure you want to put your money at risk in this way?

So why do people do it? It's exciting. It's riveting. In fact, it's very much akin to gambling. I don't know much about online poker, but my sense is that it's driven by the same mentality. It's the idea of sitting alone in your apartment or your second bedroom, staring at a computer screen and trying to beat the other guy.

But people who play online poker are probably much better at poker than day traders are at investing. With poker, there are real strategies, and if you spend enough time at it, you can get really good. With day trading, it's all but impossible to beat the market over the long term. So if you're really that excited about going online and trying to make a few dollars, I would say take some poker lessons. You'll have a lot more fun.

There's one more thing to consider about day trading versus buying the market: compound interest. With day trading, you're up, you're down, you're up again, and you're down again. But when you keep your money in the market, it basically doubles every seven years at the historical 10 percent annualized return—as it has done for the past forty-nine years. If you do the math (and I'll show you how in a later chapter), you'll see that you could've made 120 times your money by keeping it in an index fund over the last forty-nine years . . . while with day trading, good luck. Who knows what you would've made? Not that much.

An index fund offers a mind-boggling return, but you've got to stay in there. You cannot take profits, and therefore you won't have to pay taxes—unlike day traders, who have to pay taxes on every successful investment. Your accumulation of wealth is phenomenal, all because you just sat there and let the money roll in. Will you get the adrenaline boost that you get from day trading if you stick your money in the market and leave it in? Of course not. But you already know how I feel about that.

Commodities

Let's turn now to another hot topic—commodities. Wherever you turn, you see ads exhorting you to invest in gold and other commodities, either as a means of making money or as a hedge. So the question is to what extent, if any, should you include gold or any other precious metal or commodity in your investment portfolio?

Let me preface the discussion by sharing with you a fact that the commodities industry would not like you to know: When I was a broker, I would do a little bit of commodity trading for my clients, and I was shocked at how high the commissions were. On a fifty-thousand-dollar account, I could generate a thousand dollars' worth of commissions on any given day. In other words, the commodities market is geared to make *advisors* a lot of money. How will the clients do? Who cares! That seems to be the attitude of the commodities market.

For my clients who requested that I invest in gold or other commodities, the results were never good, and eventually they all asked to get out. They didn't lose much—they got out without really being burned—but I was never able to make real money for my clients in commodities, and I don't believe you should try to make your fortune from them, either.

Commodities trading is much more of a professional market than stocks or bonds. Let's say you have a contract to ship a hundred million dollars' worth of goods to Germany or France. As a commodity hedge, I might sell €90 million worth of those same goods. That way, I won't be exposed to any risk if the euro goes up or down. Commodities trading really exists as a hedge to lock in a price for people who are selling huge amounts of goods. That way, any changes in price going forward won't affect their profit or loss.

The same is true for farm commodities. Let's say someone got a deal to sell hog bellies at a certain price today, but he doesn't get paid or have to make delivery for six months. This is very common. That person will want to lock in the price he got today, because that way, his price is built into whatever expenses he may have. If the price drops in the future, he will be paid less by the person buying the commodity, but he will have locked in the sale price today. If this is your line of work, then hedging by buying or selling commodities is a sensible thing to do. That's not speculation—that's just smart business. You're guaranteeing the price in the future to cover the cost of making a deal today that involves future delivery. That's actually why commodities are sometimes called futures.

Now let's talk about you and me. Are you selling a hundred million dollars' worth of plutonium to Germany? Probably not. Do you have a contract to buy fifty million dollars' worth of hog bellies six months from today? I didn't think so. That doesn't make you a bad person. It just means that you're not a good candidate for commodities trading. This is something to be left to the professionals. It's a little like playing in traffic on the highway—chances are, you're going to get hit by a truck before you get to the other side. Speculating on whether the price of hog bellies will be higher or lower in six months just isn't a game for the average investor.

Gold and silver are the most commonly held commodities for individuals. It's true that in times of turmoil, gold tends to go up. But now you have to decide what percentage of your assets you want tied up in gold. Certainly, over the past fifty years, the stock market has returned a whole lot more than the price of gold. Should you buy gold as a hedge in case the stock market goes down? Or in case there's another major disaster? Again, you have to ask who makes money in these circumstances. Like you, I've heard ads for decades touting gold as a hedge against natural disasters, wars, and so on. But somehow, the world keeps muddling through pretty much everything, and all those people who squirreled away gold in their portfolios just lost money compared with the people who trusted the market. If you think you're going to need the secure value of gold in the future, that's your business. But I've never done it.

By the way, the gold they sell you on television is pure junk. You are buying low-quality gold—not the gold bars you see in photos of Fort Knox. I can just recall one instance of a friend who wanted to buy actual gold. I shipped it to him when he was visiting California, because in New York he would have had to pay New York State retail tax on it. My friend actually took delivery of the gold. He wanted to put forty thousand dollars in gold, so I accommodated him. I have no idea what he did with it. Is it in a safe deposit box somewhere? Did he forget where he put it? Did he lose it in a move? Who knows.

If you want to think about the performance of gold over the long term, let's go back to 1968. Back then, gold was thirty-five dollars an ounce. Yes, it has kept pace with inflation, but it has not been nearly as productive as the index. It hasn't been a great asset class. On top of that, sometimes people pay a premium for special gold coins. If the coins are rare, or if they are of particular value to collectors, they will cost more. But gold is gold. At the end of the day, the real value of a gold coin is not in what collectors will pay for it; it's the value of the metal once the coin is melted down. So if you're buying old US gold coins that are uncirculated or are especially attractive, you are paying a premium that you may not make back, even if the price of gold goes up. Benjamin Franklin's picture on the coin does not mean it is worth anything.

To come back to one of the main selling points about gold—that it will benefit you in case the world enters a state of turmoil—you have to ask what good it will do you even then. Are you going to take a gold bar down to the grocery store and buy a loaf of bread? People never think that scenario through. They just buy into the fear that those ads create. Again, you've got to ask, who makes the money? In my experience, it's not the investor. It's the salesman.

Investing Internationally

Another investment opportunity that appeals to people is to look at other parts of the world. There are lots of China funds. There are lots of funds that invest in India or Australia or Europe, or any other part of the world. If the euro is up 20 percent over two years, you're going to make a lot money. If the Chinese economy is strong, same thing.

But betting on regions is risky. For the last few years, the United Kingdom has been held hostage to the Brexit crisis. The Chinese economy is so opaque that it's hard to know exactly what is going on. Do you really want to tie your hard-earned money to the fortunes of regions outside the United States? To me, it just seems like too much risk.

At the same time, as much as 35 percent of the revenue that American companies create comes from sales overseas. We sell a lot of iPhones and Fords and vacuum cleaners and yes, SodaStream machines all over the planet. So by buying the US market, you are actually benefitting from growth in the markets in other countries as well. There are a lot of mutual funds that specialize in overseas investment, but picking the right one is not easy. And then on top of that, you've got the fee structure and all the other costs of investing in funds, which we have discussed in previous chapters. It's not necessary to gild the lily. If you buy the QQQ, or the Dow Jones, or the S&P, you will, in fact, be making an investment in the whole world.

I'm not in a position to compare investing in the market with buying certain forms of insurance, investing in fine art, or other asset classes or investments. At the risk of sounding like a broken record, all I know is that the stock market has returned more money to people than any other investment class, if they buy and hold, if they don't pay for advice, and if they buy the market. Should you do anything else with your money? As you get older, you do want to put an increasing proportion of your investments into bonds or other fixed income assets that pay higher returns. The older you are, the less risk you probably want to run. You can pay for that advice or you can go online and figure it out for yourself. It's not that complicated. As for fine art, yes, it has made people a lot of money, but only at the super high-end level. Most people with a million dollars to invest are not going to spend half of that on a piece of art. It's probably not wise.

At the same time, live your life. If you want to buy a second home for family vacations, buy it and enjoy it! If there's a Matisse that you love and you can afford it, buy the Matisse and hang it on your wall! Enjoy yourself! But just remember that these things may or may not pan out as investments over the long term. Can you tell your friends at the club or the cocktail party a great story about the fact that your Matisse is rising 12 percent a year? Of course. Matisse has been terrific on the market over the last half century!

But I'm not here to advise you to make esoteric investments. I'm here to talk about meat and potatoes. And remember that in each of the things that we're talking about, whether it's day trading, commodities, currency speculation, investing directly in other parts of the world, or anything else, there's always going to be somebody standing between you and your money—and *that* person is guaranteed to make money. You? Not so much.

* * *

Financial advice is like bottled water. In most parts of the country, tap water is perfectly fine. But the bottled water industry has convinced us that the impurities in tap water are going to kill us, so everybody goes around with expensive plastic bottles of water. And often, the bottled water is just as impure as the tap water! It's no healthier! They've run tests that prove this. And yet, everyone is convinced that they need bottled water to stay alive. People are paying a premium for something that they don't need.

In financial services, it's the same thing, but instead of bottled water, they're selling advice. You don't need advice any more than you need bottled water. I don't believe I'm going to be able to dislodge you from your bottled water habit if you already have one, but that's not the purpose of this book. I am trying to dislodge you from the idea that you need to pay for advice. Each of the investments in this chapter requires you to pay for advice, pay higher taxes, pay fees and commissions, or all of the above. For what? A better story to tell at the club?

I'm not here to help you formulate a fabulous investment story; I am here to help you create great returns. And with the money you make on your index fund, you can buy all the bottled water you want! How does that sound?

CHAPTER 7

Financial "News" Networks Can Be Hazardous to Your Wealth

Consider for a moment what a typical TV financial "news" program looks like. Just think about the screen for a minute. On the right? News headlines flashing so quickly you can barely process the information they contain. At the bottom of the screen? Not one but two or sometimes even three "crawls"—current statistics of what stocks, bonds, commodities, indexes, and whatever else they can think of are selling for right this second.

What do you care? You have a buy-and-hold-forever strategy. Who cares whether Apple is up three points or Facebook is down two points? What are you going to do, call your broker and yell, "Sell!" as if you were in some 1940s black-and-white movie about the stock market?

And what's even funnier is that if they run out of stocks and bonds to report on, they will have a crawl dedicated to sports scores. What are people doing, investing in commodities and then getting down bets on hockey games? It's a joke.

Then you see an announcer, very nicely dressed, as if that person has somewhere important to go. That person has nowhere to go. All he or she is going to do is sit there and feed you information—in an excited, agitated tone, guaranteed to make you feel as though you have to get up and do something. Did you hear what she said? Tesla is going to miss its estimates! Boeing is trying to figure out how to make safe jets that don't fall out of the sky! Really! Who knew? But more to the point, why do you care?

We are conditioned to assume that if a person is speaking to us in an authoritative tone, with great energy and certainty, we have to get up and do something about it. That's what they want you to think! They're trying to get you to buy into complexity. And as they talk, those crawls are still going by underneath, and those headlines are still floating to the side.

It's like being at a slot machine in Vegas, with all the noise and froth that make you want to sit there and keep pumping in your hard-earned money. At least in a casino, you can call it "entertainment." I don't think there's anything entertaining about watching financial TV, or about losing money based on the agitation of emotions that follows from watching those shows.

Finally, the announcer will bring in a special guest: a top executive at some important company. Great! Now you can get the latest news about the company and make a brilliant investment decision based on that news! Except for one thing. Never in the history of financial services television has any CEO *ever* come on a show and said something that was newsworthy. They only say things that are already well-known to the investing community, and therefore already baked into the stock price. It's pure hype.

They're telling you how great their companies are, how great their management is, how great their new products are, whatever. They're salesmen and saleswomen. They have a product to sell, and that is their stewardship of their companies. They want you to see how brilliant they are. They want you to believe that they've got everything figured out, and it wouldn't be the worst thing if you bought some stock, because that would help drive up their stock price. So don't think of it as news. Understand exactly what it really is—advertising. Or as they used to say on the boardwalk in Atlantic City, it's shilling for their stock.

So what do people do when they see these beautifully dressed, well-spoken, smooth CEOs talking about how great their companies are? That's right. They invest. But they're way behind the market. They're fools, and not Motley Fools. Just the plain old simple kind of fool that nobody wants to be. But they watch those shows, they get agitated instead of educated, and then they vote with their dollars. And typically, you guessed it, they vote wrong.

If you tune in between 9:00 a.m. and 9:30 a.m. on CNBC, you will actually see a countdown to the opening bell of the NY Stock Exchange, in minutes and seconds, at the bottom right-hand corner of the screen. What are they going to do at the NY Stock Exchange? Launch a rocket to the moon? It's just another day of trading. Even that countdown to the opening bell increases the sense of excitement, froth, and motivation to take action. I can assure you in all of the decades I worked in financial services we never sat there at the office, breathlessly counting down the seconds until the market opened. All this does is feed into the sense of Vegas-like excitement and anticipation, causing people to react emotionally instead of responding intellectually. If you're caught up in how many seconds there are until the opening bell, you are practically guaranteed to give up possible index return. The stock market rewards those who think in terms of years or even decades—not those who breathlessly count down minutes and seconds.

These shows are addictive. All those crawls and headlines and announcers and guests are there to keep you in a state of emotional excitement, so that you'll keep watching. That helps their ratings. It doesn't help your life. The only thing that really matters is whether the market as a whole went up or down on any given day. You can find out that piece of information in a split second on your phone.

If you really need to watch the financial services television programs, go ahead. But just wait until you get the information about the Standard & Poor's, and then turn the thing off. Or watch something that's real entertainment, like a good movie or a good TV series. The short of it is that there's nothing beneficial about watching these programs, so why bother?

Of all the programs on financial news networks, the one that troubles me the most is Jim Cramer's show, *Real Money*. I have to acknowledge my personal bias in this matter, because he loved SodaStream on the way up and then trashed the company, based on zero information, when the price began to drop. So I'll do my best to set aside that personal bias—because of the way he disrespected a stock that was so important to my clients and me—as I share with you my thoughts about his approach.

Cramer's show is all about engaging the viewer and investing in the moment. He is shrill and dramatic, which makes him appropriate viewing for many. But his approach is the opposite of long-term profitable investing. Is he entertaining, with the sound effects, lights, and herky-jerky camera style? Obviously. It's a lot more entertaining than buying and holding an index fund, which is a snooze fest. It's like watching grass grow. That's the problem—Cramer is so entertaining that he gives people the absolutely wrong idea about what investing really is.

It blows my mind that so many people entrust their financial futures to a man who honks horns and rings bells. His show has nothing to do with news, let alone news about the financial world or the stock market. It's reality television—in the sense that it creates a reality more exciting than actual reality. His show is no different from those other "reality shows" where they put eight people in a home in order to foster confrontation. It makes arresting television. But arresting television doesn't mean you are receiving good investment advice.

I don't want to make this a book about SodaStream, but my sense is that what Jim Cramer did with that company is emblematic of how he handles pretty much all companies. His modus operandi, as we've seen, is to ride a stock on the way up, as a momentum investor, and then dump it as soon as it starts to show weakness. He was treating SodaStream, like almost every stock he discusses, as a piece of paper and not as an actual company with products, customers, a management team, and a bright future. So here's what he did.

He loved the company on the way up, and then came that long stretch where only the most faithful of investors stayed with the stock. Not him. For the next five years, he panned SodaStream every chance he could. Bad stock. Bad stock. Bad stock. Sell. Sell. Sell.

One particular moment stands out, and perhaps all these recollections indicate that I have spent too much time watching Jim Cramer! When SodaStream dropped back to 50 from 70, Cramer went on a rant about how SodaStream management didn't know what they were doing. He suggested that SodaStream management was negligent for demanding certain kinds of placement for its product in Target stores. According to Cramer, that was horrible. You can't tell Target what to do! I sat there scratching my head and asking myself, On what basis is Cramer making these pronouncements? He's not on the management team. He's not involved in negotiations with Target. He obviously picked up a bit of industry gossip from somewhere. But did he verify it? A true journalist never goes to print or on the air with a news item from a single source. Without confirmation, it's rumor, not a story. But not in Cramer land. Anything he heard, or anything he thought, was fair game.

About a year later, Coca-Cola took a 10 percent stake in Keurig. They invested a billion dollars and announced that they were going into the do-it-yourself home soda market. Cramer knew nothing more about Keurig's products than he did about SodaStream's. That didn't stop him from predicting that Keurig, backed by Coca-Cola, would crush SodaStream. It certainly looked that way at the moment. SodaStream was about $35 a share at the time, and Keurig's share price jumped up 20 percent because of Coca-Cola making that investment. Keurig actually went up to around 130 over the next six months, but it was pure froth. Keurig failed, and if Cramer had been the slightest bit curious, he could have quickly learned the reasons why . . . and even shared them on his show.

The Keurig machine costs $350, instead of $70 for the SodaStream machine. Reviewers said it sounded like a snow-plow when you turned it on, and it took four or five hours to bring the water temperature down to a drinkable level of forty or forty-five degrees. To put it simply, it was a miserable product. A dog. But Cramer didn't know that. He didn't know anything. He just went ahead and talked about how Keurig was changing the market because now you could make all these branded sodas—indeed, even Coca-Cola—at home. Of course, it turned out that nobody wanted to make sodas at home! All they wanted was an easy, economical way to make seltzer! Nuances like that were lost on Cramer.

Whenever there was a mention of SodaStream on Cramer's show, it was negative. It was a stock to be avoided. Finally, in 2018, Pepsi bought SodaStream at $144 a share—almost five times what it was worth when he declared that the Keurig home soda system would bury SodaStream.

But did Cramer admit that his judgment had been wrong? No . . . he just said that at this price it was a good deal for Pepsi to diversify into the water end of the drink market.

This is how Kramer dealt with his frightening prediction that the Keurig home soda system, backed by the Coca-Cola brand, would destroy SodaStream. Basically he claimed for the fifth time in five years that SodaStream was the worst! So much for the Jim Cramer prediction.

Keurig wrote off several hundred million dollars on its killer attempt to catch SodaStream. Cramer was wrong, and he just ignored his previous statement—because it proved his analysis had been wrong. Don't say a word . . . just praise Pepsi for buying SodaStream at $144 a share.

Sometimes you may get the feeling that I'm obsessed with SodaStream! And you might be right. I spent so many years with that stock, hanging in there when the rest of the world turned its back on it, which only made the payoff that much sweeter when it finally arrived. The reason I tell this story in so much detail is because I believe it is representative of the way Cramer operates. He knows little or nothing about the companies he touts or condemns. He spins a tiny bit of information, accurate or otherwise, into a firm prediction about what's going to happen next. He sounds so authoritative that you feel you have no choice but to believe him. And the guy can certainly command an audience. He's been on the air for years, and no one seems to call him out on his practices, which fall, in my opinion, far below the level of journalistic integrity. In short, Cramer is a showman, an entertainer. You wouldn't take stock tips from your favorite comedian on *The Tonight Show*, so why are you taking them from a guy running around with bells, whistles, flashing lights, and no facts?

Cramer's focus is relentlessly short-term. If something is up 20 percent in one day, he has to talk about it. He tends toward what's called momentum investing, which has been proven to be ineffective. He will recommend any stock that has taken a fairly recent jump upwards. And once it stops jumping, he reverses himself and becomes negative. He comes across as so knowledgeable and persuasive, not to mention energetic and entertaining, that viewers tend to believe he knows everything about everything. But that's just simply impossible. On Wall Street, you cannot know everything about more than a few items of focus. Cramer epitomizes the concept of a little knowledge being a dangerous thing. It's dangerous to your financial life to think short term, to try to coast on upward moves, or to try to outsmart the market. Believe me, the market is much smarter than any of us, even Jim Cramer.

The opposite of momentum investing is value investing, where we look for stocks with prices that do not reflect the long-term prospects of the company. Value investing goes back to the founders of modern investment thinking, Graham and Dodd. You can read their textbook, written decades ago, which is hundreds of pages long. And essentially what you'll discover is that you want to look for stocks representing companies with futures much brighter than their current stock prices might suggest. But reading Graham and Dodd is boring for most people, and so is the work it takes to find such companies to invest in, compared with the shock and awe of a half an hour with Jim Cramer. He comes across as the viewer's best friend.

I'm not denying his showmanship. I am saying that you don't make your decisions about how to conduct your relationships based on a house of eight strangers depicted in reality TV. So why would you make your investment decisions based on the same kind of show?

If you asked me whether a stock is going to be up or down next year, I wouldn't presume to guess. If I knew enough about it, I could tell you where it's going to be in twenty years. It'll be higher, if it's still around, because things grow over time. But next year? Six months from now? A year from now? Two years from now? I wouldn't begin to touch something like that. No one can possibly know. The joke is that economists and weather forecasters get paid whether they are correct or incorrect. The same thing is true with the Jim Cramers of the world. They make their money regardless of how much money you may lose. Interestingly, Cramer doesn't just report the "news"—he becomes the news. If he mentions a stock, other people will report that Cramer is excited about that particular investment. His opinion becomes news itself, because it is given in a news-like format.

To my knowledge, no one has tried to determine what his track record might be. But we know for a certainty that momentum investing doesn't work. Once Cramer says something, though, everybody else jumps on the bandwagon.

Can his utterances move the market? A little bit. For a very short moment. But not enough for his followers to make money. It's also worth remembering that his show is really a thirty-minute infomercial for his stock-picking service. But whether he sends you an email that tells you to buy or sell, or says the same thing on the show—honking horns, running around, flashing lights, pushing buttons that create sound effects—it's the same thing. It's a person who appears to know more than you do, but doesn't.

Is the show titillating? Of course. But the stock market is about money and business. It shouldn't be titillating—and until the development of shows like Cramer's, it never was. The only thing that should be exciting about investing is opening your statements years from now and seeing how much your investments have gone up. On a day-to-day basis, if you want excitement, run a 5K. Go to an adventure movie. Try a new restaurant. But don't risk your financial future in the name of quick returns and emotional highs.

Often, the general advice Cramer provides, not just about one particular stock but about investing in general, is dead wrong. I've heard him say that you never go wrong when you take a profit. I believe the exact opposite is true! Taking profit is one of the worst things you can do in the market. You're going to miss out on the future growth of a company you've identified as successful and growing—and on top of that, you'll have to pay tax.

Holding onto profits for as long as possible is where the money is made. Intelligent investors know that. Taking a profit, as counterintuitive as it sounds, is a terrible philosophy, and yet that's precisely what Cramer advocates. Taking profits inhibits potential growth. The worst mistakes I've ever made as an investor haven't involved losses. They've involved future profits I gave up when I sold too soon.

There's only one place where it's a good idea to take a profit and walk away, and that's called a casino. If you make money at the craps table or by playing blackjack, get out of there! Eventually you will lose. We all know that in casinos, the house always wins. A lot of people say that the stock market is a casino, but only if you treat it as one. If you treat it as a serious place where you go to invest long term, you'll be fine. In a casino, you never go wrong taking a profit. That's exactly what you should do if you are lucky enough to be ahead at any given time! Take your money off the table. Go have a nice dinner, see a show, or buy yourself or a loved one a present with your winnings. But get out before your luck changes and the inevitable occurs. If Cramer were giving you advice about how to bet in a casino, I would have to agree with him. But not in the stock market.

Cramer gives you the sense that investing is a board game. What's the difference between his show and *Wheel of Fortune* or *Family Feud*? The only difference is that on those shows, you're watching people make fools of themselves trying to win a lawnmower or maybe a new car. I wish them luck! I hope they all win! But there's a big difference between a game show mentality and the mindset of a successful investor. If you lose on *Wheel of Fortune*, life goes on. If you lose out on what could have been a comfortable retirement, well, that's serious business.

As long as we're talking about people for whom I have little regard, let's talk about Bill O'Reilly. The former Fox News pundit was tossed off the air, as you may recall, because of all his inappropriate behavior toward women who worked for his show. You may wonder where O'Reilly has been ever since. If you are a stock market gambler—I would not use the word *investor* in this context—then you certainly know where he has been. He is now shilling for a guy who touts various stocks. O'Reilly actually shows up at his events. I get emails about this all the time.

The investor employing Bill O'Reilly promises fabulous returns, and since Bill O'Reilly is backing him, lots of people must figure that the guy knows what he's talking about. It's crazy. What makes Bill O'Reilly an authority about the stock market? Certainly he's making plenty of money in the market, but only in fees for showing up at these events. My feeling is that O'Reilly has time on his hands and he likes being in the spotlight. So now he gets paid to be out there in front of people, like a sideshow carnival barker. It's just undignified. He's working for a guy who touts $3 stocks. Those sorts of investments are appealing to a certain mentality: people who believe they can get rich quick. But there's a reason why certain stocks sell for $3, or a $1.50, or whatever. It's because the market thinks very little of them, short term or long term. It's just one more way to separate money from the pockets of the gullible. So whether it's Jim Cramer, Bill O'Reilly, or anyone else trying to get between you and your hard-earned investment dollars, I hope you will be smart enough to place your hand over your wallet and keep moving. They are advocating a fool's game.

Just this morning, I turned on CNBC to see what they were talking about. The headline: *50 Stocks For You to Follow Right Now.* You can imagine how I felt when I saw that headline! Almost nauseated! I've said this over and over because I want to lock this idea in for you. No one can follow fifty stocks. Not a professional, not an amateur investor. Nobody. But I am a lone voice in the wilderness, compared with the thousands of financial services websites, books, magazines, television programs, and marketing materials with the sole purpose of convincing you that making money in the market is a complicated task.

As I was working on this chapter, I saw an article in *Financial Press* tying changes in stock market prices to interest rate moves by the Federal Reserve. The article suggests that stocks are "overvalued"—their prices are too high and are likely to take a tumble. How on earth can a reporter who writes about the Federal Reserve have secret insight into the appropriate pricing of stocks? The term *overvalued* implies that if the market had a brain in its head, it would drop substantially so that stocks were priced appropriately. This kind of assertion is upsetting to me because, as I've said time and again in these pages, no one can possibly predict what can happen in the short term. Over the long term, the market has always gone up and almost certainly will continue to do so. There's never been an economic engine for growth quite like the United States of America. So I'm very confident about the long term.

My question for the reporter who wrote that article is this: If he's so smart why is he a newspaper reporter? If he's so confident in his assertions about where the market is headed, why isn't he spending all of his time raising money from family, friends, and the general public to bet against the current pricing of stocks? It's important for the average investor to take a lesson from this sort of story. I'm not suggesting the reporter lacks intelligence. I am saying that people like him are assuming a mantle of authority to which they have no real right. Who knows what the market is going to do? This guy? If that's how you feel, then short the market. But don't come crying to me because you listened to his advice instead of mine.

Okay, we've talked about TV financial "news"—and how detrimental it can be to your financial well-being. In the next chapter, we'll look at other ways the financial advice industry tries to separate you from your hard-earned cash.

CHAPTER 8

They Want You to Think Investing's Complicated— Don't Buy the Lie

The financial services industry has spent billions of dollars brainwashing people into thinking that the market is incredibly complex. So let me give you an example from another industry that you and I know all too well—the diet industry.

We all know the key to losing weight: Eat better, don't eat junk, move more. It's so simple. But every January, you go to the bookstore and what do you see? Front and center, a section called "New Year, New You." Everybody's number one New Year's resolution is to lose weight. Unfortunately, most of us end up weighing more on December 31 than we did back on New Year's Day!

Most people who buy diet books have already bought other diet books. Why are they buying a second, third, fourth, or fifth diet book? Because they don't want to go through the real stress and effort it takes to lose weight. They think that if they eat a pound of broccoli every day for thirty days, because this book tells them to, or if they stop eating this and start eating that, they will find the magic key. They will lose the weight without having to make any real changes in their lives. That's what people are shopping for when they buy multiple diet books over a period of time—the easy way out.

What would it take to lose weight? Keep it simple. Don't overcomplicate things. Recognize that there is a whole billion-dollar industry offering diet books, diet plans, snack foods, point systems, and whatever, all of which may or may not take any inches off your waistline but will surely take cash out of your pocket. As always, I'm not here to tell you what to do with your life. You want to eat ice cream every night and be fifty pounds overweight, that's your prerogative. It's a free country. But if you want to do the right thing for your body, you know what to do. Keep it simple. Ignore the overcomplications that the diet industry thrives on. Just do what you know is the right thing to do—eat less, exercise more.

What's the difference between the financial services industry and the diet book industry? Not so much. Both thrive on making you believe that everything is so complicated that you need to rely on their help instead of a simple plan. If everybody ate better and exercised more, the diet book publishers would go out of business. Similarly, if everyone accepted the idea that there is a simpler way to make money in the stock market, and that they don't have to fall for the overcomplications of the financial services industry, they would be a lot better off.

The difference is that it's easy to grasp the concept of "eat less, eat better, exercise more." It's just logical. Everybody understands that. When it comes to investing, though, there's nothing intuitive about the simple approach I am suggesting. There's no way that an individual without any training in the market could possibly understand and embrace this approach. How would you know what an ETF is? How would you know where to buy it? How would you know to buy that and not everything that they're talking about in the financial services media?

Just as you learn the correct way to diet without more advice, you will never need another lesson in "how to beat the market" after you've read this book. It teaches how to invest through index-based investment.

That's the proper way—the *only* way—to invest in the market. This book provides the perfect regimen. It is "the perfect stock market diet."

Now relax! Game over!

As an experiment, I decided to subscribe to two of the most highly regarded financial services websites, Jim Cramer and Motley Fool. I said to myself, I'm mentioning these names in my book. I ought to know what they're doing. As soon as

I signed up, I found myself bombarded with information about twenty different stocks from each of them. One of the primary recommendations was to sell DuPont and buy something called TWLO. I didn't even know what TWLO was. I thought maybe it was a TV series. It turned out to be a high tech company of some sort that I'd never heard of. As for the DuPont recommendation, Cramer had recommended it six months ago, but it had not gone anywhere. So now they were recommending selling it.

Just because DuPont didn't move doesn't mean the market as a whole stood still. So any well-meaning investor who took the advice that Cramer and Motley Fool were offering, and bought stocks that went nowhere, might not have lost any money. But they certainly did not enjoy the gain that they would've experienced had they simply put their money into an index fund and left it there. On top of that, they didn't experience the benefit of compound interest that they would've enjoyed (which I will explain in detail shortly) had they kept their money in an index fund and not gotten confused by Motley Fool and Cramer.

My subscription to Cramer's service set me back $350 for the first year. (Trust me, there won't be a second year.) Three-hundred fifty dollars is not that much money to me. But if you have a $100,000 portfolio, that $350 equals thirty-five "basis points," which is three times the price of buying an index fund. That's real money! That same money could have been invested in an index fund. Instead, you aren't getting any richer, but Cramer certainly is.

In addition, my sense is that most of the people picking up his service don't have $2 million or $3 million portfolios. The bigger the portfolio, the smaller the relative cost of the investment in his "advice." Most people in our society aren't rich, and $350 is real money. What are you getting for that real money? Complexity. Confusion. Advice on stocks that won't beat the index. Or if the stock is successful enough to go up a little, Cramer or Motley Fool will recommend that you sell to take profit off the table. In that case, maybe you lucked into a stock that was headed for even greater success. But now you've cut yourself off from that growth, too.

Let's go back to the diet and exercise comparison. Most people don't like to go to the gym. Most people don't like to work out. Doing fifty pushups is a lot of effort. Making one phone call, or going online to make an investment in an index fund, is a heck of a lot easier than doing fifty pushups! You can even have a pastry when you're done. What do I care! So not only is making money in the market simple, but it's actually easier than working out! You can take the money you would've spent on a gym membership, or Weight Watchers, and invest that in an ETF! And then go have a cannoli. You've earned it.

Similarly, if you really commit to eating properly, you'll never need to read another diet book as long as you live. You've already grooved new habits. You eat the right thing and you don't have dessert, or two desserts. When you go shopping, you buy healthy foods. You don't give in to impulse purchases at the supermarket, 7-Eleven, or anywhere. So what do you need another diet book for? A paperweight?

The same thing is true with investing in index funds. Once you make the plunge, you don't need to read any more books on investing. You don't need to watch Cramer or any of the other financial services shows. You don't need to subscribe to services. You can go out in the sunshine and take a nice walk. Hear the birds chirp. See lovers holding hands in the park. *Be a lover holding hands in the park.* These are the wonderful experiences that await once you break your addiction to complexity and novelty, which are the two things that keep most people stuck to their masters in the financial services industry, and quite frankly, stuck in reverse. Better still, now you'll have the money to go out and hire someone to do those fifty pushups for you!

You might say, "But Gene, aren't I supposed to be an educated investor?" I suppose, but does it really matter what the president tweets? Or what General Motors or Facebook does? You already own those stocks in your ETF. You've already bought the stocks that they're talking about. You're not going to be selling off a piece of your ETF just because you hear something negative about General Motors. Look, General Motors has been around for a long time. They'll figure it out. Now, I'm not suggesting that anything that they say is fraudulent or even inaccurate. I'm just saying it's irrelevant.

Let's take Facebook or Amazon. These are basically one or two companies out of the five hundred in the S&P. Granted, Facebook and Amazon will have a bigger impact on your fund than a tiny company. But what do you care about what one company is doing when you own a piece of five hundred companies? Not one of those enterprises, not even Facebook or Amazon, equates to 3 percent of the overall index. Think of each of those stocks as one tree in a forest. While none of those trees will ever grow to the sky, and some of them might get wiped out, for the most part, the rest are just going to grow. Not in an exciting manner. Not in a manner that will command the headlines. But instead, they will just keep going up and up. So focus on the overall forest, and don't worry about the individual trees.

One of the most foolish mistakes an individual investor can make is to look at the news and try to make a guess as to what is going to happen next. Back in 2016, half of America thought the world had ended with the election of President Donald Trump. I'm not here to talk about politics or to get into a debate about what you think about him. What no one can deny is that the market has gone up over 40 percent since he took office, and that's just three years into his first term. You can think he is the greatest statesman since George Washington or you can think he's a deranged lunatic. But if you had told yourself, "Trump is in, so the economy's going to collapse," and then acted on that premise, look how much gain you would have missed. Vote however you like. Watch Fox News or CNN. Read the *National Review* or the *New Republic*. Whatever floats your boat politically. But if you had tried to make a bet on your financial future based on the headlines? You would've missed out on one of the biggest moves in the history of the market. And you would have nobody to blame but yourself.

What happens if a Democrat with socialist tendencies becomes president? Will the market suddenly tank? Who knows? There's no such thing as an uncracked crystal ball. Making bets—and that's all it really is—based on your expectations of what a president will or will not do is, more often than not, the road to financial underperformance. Okay, that's a little strong. But it's certainly a road map to you sitting still while everybody else is galloping ahead.

Another thing to consider, when you watch financial news, is that it isn't really news. It's entertainment. Decades ago, the news divisions of each of the three major networks were not there to make money. They were essentially a public service, and their goal was to report the news as they saw fit. Maybe they had something of a liberal bias, but they were still sincere and whole-hearted in their desire to inform you. Today, that's history. Television news *is* entertainment. It's all about ratings. The line between news and entertainment has been obliterated.

Television news is made to attract and entertain viewers, and coverage of the stock market is the exact same thing.

When I look at the people who are anchors and so-called analysts on television news, I have to laugh—because otherwise, I would cry. These individuals were trained first as performers, and then as newscasters, and finally as financial analysts who, at least theoretically, understand the market. Of course, they understand the overall concept of what a stock market is. But they don't have the slightest idea of what really makes the most money. If they did, they would be sitting home investing, instead of getting dressed every day and putting on a nice outfit and makeup and looking serious, concerned, and agitated as they present the "financial news." Some of them have a very sedate, news-like delivery, and others are very provocative and excited—sometimes as they are describing the very same event. Is this good for your bottom line? You tell me. The whole package encourages short-term thinking, and as we've seen over and over again, short-term thinking is dangerous to your ongoing financial health.

I want to come back to Motley Fool for a moment. One of the claims that they make is that over the past five years, the market was up 85 percent, but their stocks are up 350 percent. I don't believe it. There's no way that's possible. You cannot have a fifteen stock portfolio that's up 350 percent when the market is only up 85 percent. You cannot get quadruple the return with a portfolio of twelve to fifteen stocks. They'll tell you things like, "We recommended Netflix when it was $5 a share, and now it's $300." I call that getting lucky. When Netflix was $5 a share, were they telling all of their followers to sell everything else and buy Netflix? Of course not! Netflix was just one stock of many that they were recommending. And if a stock didn't move fast enough, they would tell people to sell, and would plug another one in.

The people running Motley Fool are making money month after month, year after year. But what about their investors? So that's why I'm really unhappy about an advertisement that says they are up 350 percent over a period of time when the market was up 85 percent. If it sounds too good to be true, it is, even if it's a trusted brand like Motley Fool that's doing the talking. Over the course of the time it took Netflix to rise from $5 a share to $300, Motley Fool most likely recommended another five hundred stocks. Do you think all of those went up sixty times? Of course not. It's that old line—there are lies, damned lies, and statistics. Motley Fool, like any of the financial services firms, cherry-picks its numbers to make them look better than they are. It's not rocket science. It's not science of any kind. It's science fiction.

Let's get away from these subscription services and focus our attention on financial advisors. They also promote complexity. Their message: "You're on your own. You don't have our researchers. You don't have our resources. You don't have our history of studying the market. We're able to put together a portfolio of fifty to one hundred stocks that should outperform the index. (Will it? Nineteen out of twenty times, it won't, but they're not going to tell you that. But that doesn't matter to them. As long as they can make you think they are smarter than you are, they win.) They are cultivating in you a sense of uncertainty, because they may not offer returns, but they certainly offer a sense of certainty. Why are you paying for the illusion of certainty when you could be making more money?

The financial services firms and their advisors also spend a great deal of time, effort, and money to convince you that they can get you whatever specific returns you are looking for. Maybe it's dividends. Maybe it's growth. Maybe it's a combination of the two. Only one problem—all of those things exist in ETFs, at a much cheaper price. In other words, you can find ETFs that specialize in growth, and you can find ETFs that specialize in dividends. The cost for those investments will inevitably be less than that 1 percent you are paying an advisor to manage your money.

On top of that, the financial services firms typically turn over 15 percent of their portfolios a year. Why? Because all their brilliant research and "inside information" (they don't have any) is telling them to sell 15 percent of their stocks. Why do they sell the stocks? Some of them are dogs and have lost money. So they want to cut their losses. Others, as we have seen, are actually good stocks, but they're selling those in order to capture some upside and make themselves look good.

And you know what happens when they do that—you don't benefit from the continued upside if that underlying company is doing well. Again, it goes back to that mentality of looking at stocks as pieces of paper and not as something that represents ownership in an actual company with actual management, actual products and services, and actual customers.

So if a financial advisory firm is getting rid of 15 percent of the stocks they've already bought, at the end of five years, they own almost certainly less than 25 percent of the portfolio they started with. This is short-term thinking at its worst. As we've seen, the golden rule of diversification and portfolio balance, which all the major financial services firms swear by, is the enemy of making great profits. And while those guys are selling off 15 percent of their portfolios, index funds are only turning over 2 to 3 percent of their portfolios a year. And if they're doing that, they're doing it for a darned good reason. Not just simply to get rid of dogs or make themselves look good. At the end of those same five years, while your financial advisory firm's portfolio has sold off more than 75 percent of its initial holdings, the ETF is churning along, making money, and most likely holding 90 percent of its original investments.

Even people who know virtually nothing about the stock market can guess which companies have gone up the most over the last ten or twenty years. What would you say they are? If you guessed Apple, Google, Facebook, and the like, you're right. Those are the ones that have gone up the most. Apple went from a capitalization of $50 billion to a capitalization of a trillion dollars. That's twenty times growth in just twenty years. But how many money managers were allowed to keep Apple in their portfolios for that whole time? Practically none. You know the rule: diversification. Limit the risk that the financial services firm faces, even if it's going to lose money for the customers. Take profits off the table.

I would be thrilled if you could show me ten years' worth of statements from a portfolio created by a financial services firm that captured all of the growth Apple has enjoyed over the last ten years. It's going to be a very rare situation. Pretty much the only time it happens is when *the customer* insists that Apple doesn't get touched. I've heard story after story of people saying to their brokers, "Don't touch Apple!" or "Don't touch Google!" In that case, shouldn't those individuals be paying that 1 percent fee to themselves? Shouldn't the financial advisors be paying the 1 percent fee to those clients, for the excellent market advice? Just something to think about.

So we've talked about the touts and we've talked about the television shows. Let's focus for a minute on *Barron's*, *Fortune*, *Forbes*, and the *Wall Street Journal*. If you want to read those articles for news about politics, go ahead. The *Wall Street Journal* does an excellent job of covering politics. But anytime you read a story about a company, you can be sure that the market already has that information well before you do. Making investment decisions based on what you read about a stock in one of those financial newspapers or magazines is not a winning strategy. I'm a big fan of *Wall Street Journal* editorials, but that has nothing to do with my investing life. That's just a way of staying informed. You just don't have to stay abreast of the market on a constant basis. In fact, my approach is exactly the opposite of everything that you see in the world of complexity. My advice is "set and forget."

People get so consumed by whether the market was up a lot or down a lot on any given day. If you knew that fifty years from now, the market would be thirty times what it is today, why would you care if the market goes up or down 25 percent in a given year? And if you sell off, you have to pay taxes. Stay put. Leave the money in. Ignore the siren song of complexity. It's not your friend.

This next story is for any of you boys and girls out there who think you're so smart that you can outthink the market. So pull up your chairs and let me share with you the short, sad tale of Long-Term Capital Management.

The way the firm probably came into existence is that a bunch of pointy-headed geeks at MIT were sitting around The Rathskeller or wherever those very smart people hang out, and the conversation turned to the stock market. They most likely said to themselves, hey, we're really smart. Among us, we have a Nobel Prize, we have PhDs from MIT—surely the stock market would be no match for our brilliance. So they hit on the idea of creating a computer model that they figured couldn't be beat.

They noticed that there were certain discrepancies in the market that, over time, could be taken advantage of to the tune of millions of dollars. What kind of discrepancies? I would need a Nobel Prize and some PhDs from MIT to explain it, and you would need the same things to understand. Suffice it to say that these guys thought they had the whole thing figured out.

For a couple of years, they did. They were buying thirty-year bond futures with 10:1 leverage, which means that they were putting up $100,000 in order to control a million dollars' worth of bonds. Now, that's a great strategy if you're picking off those discrepancies or doing whatever smart people do in the market—and the market is going with you. And the market did go with them for a couple of years. They really thought they had everything figured out and no one could touch them.

And then reality smacked them upside the head.

The market turned against the Mensa boys at Long-Term Capital. Those discrepancies? A thing of the past. Now they were fighting an uphill battle, and they were losing rapidly—because for every hundred thousand dollars they had invested, they were actually losing money as if they had bet a million dollars. Which meant that there was a gaping hole bigger than the MIT campus in their positions.

Long-Term Capital went belly-up, and with it the idea that geniuses can outsmart the stock market. Nice try, professors. The whole thing would be humorous except for the fact that a bunch of Wall Street banks had to kick in $300 million each to buy the positions that Long-Term Capital Management had taken. If each of those ten firms hadn't sunk $300 million to buy those losing hands, the market might well have tanked, and everything we love and cherish would have gone along with it.

I tell you this story not to gloat over their arrogance, greed, and failure, but to make a point. If these guys, who have more degrees than a rectal thermometer, couldn't outsmart the market, then neither can you, ten of your best friends, or for that matter, me. The market cannot be outsmarted. The market cannot be outthought. The boys at Long-Term Capital Management took their best shot and ended up flat on their faces. They ended up having to get . . . wait for it . . . real jobs.

If you have succeeded at intellectual pursuits your whole life, kicking butt at Scrabble and crosswords in high school, acing the SATs, getting into top schools, and getting straight As on homework you did twenty minutes before class began, you may have an inflated sense of your intellectual self-worth. You may think you're really smart. In point of fact, you *are* really smart. But that doesn't mean you're going to have a better track record with the stock market than our friends at Long-Term Capital Management.

I'll say it again because it's so important. Arrogance plus greed equals disaster. That's a formula that apparently no one had thought to write on a chalkboard at MIT. It really doesn't matter how smart you are. The stock market will see you coming, eat your lunch, steal your girlfriend or boyfriend, and drive off in your car, looking back and laughing at you. If you don't believe me, go into a Wayback Machine of your own, learn the lessons of Long-Term Capital Management in greater detail—not that you need to—and then think carefully before you allow your own intellect to blind you to the complexity of the overall market.

I'm nobody's fool, but I don't have a Nobel Prize or advanced degrees from MIT. What I had was two stocks into which I poured more than two thousand hours each of research. That's roughly a year's worth of work per investment. That's how I got so lucky. The harder I worked, the luckier I got. Most investors don't have those two thousand hours, as I've said repeatedly in these pages. Chasing individual stocks is as foolish as doing what the Long-Term Capital people did. It means making bets that the house is almost guaranteed to win. Not the first day, not the second day, but over time, the house will clean you out.

What if the Long-Term Capital people had taken their winnings off the table after the first couple of years? They might have gone down as true geniuses in the annals of investing. But they couldn't do that. It's possible to create great returns for a year or two, or perhaps even three. But you cannot create off-the-chart returns year after year after year. The only people who appeared to do that were Bernie Madoff, who would make audacious claims to investors gullible enough to believe him, and a guy named Robert Schulman, who made the same kinds of claims. I had enormous respect for Schulman, who trained me at EF Hutton, but he went in a direction that I find hard to respect. He sold $3 billion (with a B!) worth of Madoff's funds to the clients of his professionally managed hedge fund, from which he profited to the tune of hundreds of millions of dollars.

The rawest recruit on Wall Street understands that you can't create outsized returns indefinitely. Surely Schulman knew what he was doing. Yet greed is a powerful intoxicant. Successful investors must always be wary of their own greed . . . and the Madoffs, Schulmans, and other Ponzi schemers looking to benefit from the greed-driven investor blinded by the chase for impossible returns.

My purpose in recounting this story is simple. Don't let your intellect, your arrogance, your greed, or any other dominant negative emotion keep you from making real money in the stock market. And unless you've got two thousand hours to invest examining the ongoing fortunes of a given company, stick to the index funds.

Getting lucky is not a retirement strategy. And that's the long (term) and short of it.

I want to share one last point with you before we close this chapter—the benefit of compounded interest. Compounded interest is a rate of return that assumes reinvestment of the money earned, back into the vehicle that earned the money. Let's say you buy a ten-year bond that yields 2 percent a year. At the end of the ten years, you have 20 percent capital that you've gotten, and you can reinvest that money. But let's say your money is in an ETF, and every time there's a dividend or gain, you buy more shares.

My 17 percent compounded return for twenty-five years turned my $100,000 investment in Timberland in 1993 into $1 million dollars by 2010. I took that million and invested it into SodaStream at $30 a share. That stock got sold to Pepsi in 2018 at $144 a share.

My initial $100,000 investment became $4.8 million dollars—a 17 percent return annually over twenty-five years. That's real money, a lot more than you can make listening to fools—Motley or otherwise!

It's a fabulous return, but it's never easy over a long investment horizon. Achieving a great return takes time and fortitude—not intelligence or luck!

Keep it simple. Keep it in an index fund or broadly based ETF. And don't buy the complexity that the financial advice industry is trying to peddle. You'll be smarter, happier, and best of all, richer.

CHAPTER 9

Getting Started with Index Investing

Getting started investing in ETFs is extraordinarily simple. There are multiple vehicles for buying what's called an index-based investment. As we've discussed, an index-based investment is a broad range of securities that mirrors going out and buying each individual security in the index—proportionate to the total dollar amount of the index it contributes.

The first of these that came into existence, and the most commonly exchange-traded fund or index fund, is SPY. This fund gives you the entire Standard & Poor's index, which means that you are investing in approximately 85 percent of the US economy. Since American companies are so deeply intertwined with the rest of the world, you are actually buying about 25 percent of the world's economy when you buy this index. As of this writing, a share of SPY costs approximately $300.

How do you buy it? Any way you want! You can buy shares of the ETF the same way you buy shares of any individual stock. You can purchase shares in a brokerage account, whether it's fee or non-fee. You can do it in a discount brokerage account. It's up to you.

The fund has returned approximately 10 percent a year since it first began in 1992. That 10 percent return is based on the expectation that investors will have reinvested any dividends they received back into the fund. SPY does not do that automatically. You have to do that yourself. Without reinvesting dividends, you would have probably made 8 percent a year. It's up to the holder to invest however he sees fit, but I don't see any better return on investment for the dividends SPY pays than putting them back into more shares of the ETF.

I want to say a word about John Bogle, founder of the Vanguard Funds. Bogle is the father of the mutual index fund, and out of all the people on Wall Street, he is the one who has had the interests of the "little guy" at heart more than anyone else. His funds are low- cost and I highly recommend them. Vanguard has a total value ETF that you can also consider. Once again, you are buying the market. Vanguard offers the Vanguard S&P fund, the "granddaddy" of all mutual index funds. It represents the S&P index. So you can buy the SPY or the Vanguard S&P index fund.

Another index ETF we've discussed, and which I regard highly, is the QQQ, which consists of the hundred largest corporations listed on the Nasdaq. The QQQ tends to be tech-oriented, because Apple trades on the Nasdaq. You will be buying a higher proportion of Apple in the QQQ than you would be in the Standard & Poor's. With any of these funds, you'll be in good shape.

Sophisticated investors sometimes wonder, "What happens if the Standard & Poor's index outperforms what the ETF is trading at?" To put it simply, that doesn't happen. If the S&P were trading at a value of a hundred, and the ETF were trading at a value of ninety-nine, this would create immediate arbitrage between people who own the stock in that ETF. They would sell the stocks, all five hundred of them, and buy the ETF. So there will never be a substantial spread between the S&P and the ETF. The arbitrage will eliminate any spread.

The good news is that if you didn't understand what I was saying in the previous paragraph, don't worry about it! That's just for folks who really need that information.

A concern about buying the QQQ is that the Nasdaq took a huge hit back in 2001, especially compared to the S&P. When the S&P index fell close to 50 percent, the Nasdaq fell over 75 percent. In other words, when the tech bubble burst back in 2001, the Nasdaq went down from 4,000 to 1,000.

But since that bottom, the Nasdaq has outperformed the S&P because it came from a lower base.

Tech companies can be boom or bust, so that creates more volatility. If you want a little more volatility, then buy the QQQ. If you want less exposure to tech, then buy the S&P. Most of the companies listed in the Nasdaq 100, which comprises the QQQ, are also included in the S&P. I have a bias toward the SPY, because it's broader.

There are plenty of other ETFs that focus on individual sectors of the market—manufacturing, aerospace, and so on. For the first time investor, my suggestion is not to make things more complicated. Don't allow your ego to think that you can pick sectors, or debate which part of the economy is going to go up more than any other part. Leave that stuff to the speculators—you, by contrast, are a true investor! Vanguard offers sector funds, which constitute about 20 percent of their business. But those funds also come with higher fees. You've got higher fees, greater risk, and for what? My advice: Stick with the S&P index fund of Vanguard. It costs 1/10 of a percent annually, and investment advisors cost a lot more—1 percent.

How much money do you put in? All you can. You want to think about the fact that you are trading consumption (buying stuff) for investment (making money on your money). If you're in your thirties or forties, put as much as you can into these index funds. As you get older and you plan to retire, you can slowly lower the equity portion and raise the fixed income portion. But if you're decades away from needing the money you are putting into a retirement account, put in as much as you possibly can.

Think of a retirement account as a gift from the government—you are able to avoid paying tax on $14,000 a year if you max out your 401(k). Let that money grow, untouched, and you'll be so happy down the road. Even if you think you can only put in $7,000 or $8,000 a year, max out. In my experience, it's shocking how many people make $250,000 a year and don't save a nickel, even when the government and their employers offer them 401(k) programs, IRAs, and the whole range of tax-advantaged investment opportunities.

If you're making $250,000 a year and spending it all on ski trips, good luck when you want to retire. But if you're able to forgo some spending—maybe get a Honda instead of a Volvo—who cares what the neighbors think? It's a lot more satisfying to watch your investment account grow instead of watching an expensive car get older, break down, and need expensive repairs. It's your choice.

Remember what I said about diet books. If you just do the right thing, you don't need to read any more diet books. It's all about grooving good habits and keeping your ego from interfering. You know that line, "Nothing tastes as good as being thin feels"? It's the same thing with the market. Nothing you can buy on Amazon or in a car dealer's showroom—or pretty much anywhere else, for that matter—will give you the long-term satisfaction of knowing that you are making money on your money, year in and year out, while you're working, while you're playing, and while you're sleeping.

My overall goal in this book has been to remove the apparent complexity from investing and to show you why you, and so many other Americans, are essentially being taken to the cleaners in financial terms year after year after year, by financial investment firms that consistently put their needs ahead of yours. What they're doing isn't illegal. It probably isn't even immoral. As I've said, I worked in that industry for decades and almost all the people I've met were decent, honest people who truly believed that they could beat the market and get a better return for their clients. Well, we all know how that story ends. Nineteen out of twenty times, it's just not possible. Were those 5 percent of advisors smarter, better educated, or better investors? Or were they just plain lucky? Good luck finding that one-in-twenty investment advisor.

Again, let me emphasize how profitable index investing is. Let's assume you are currently investing with a twenty-one-year time horizon. The minimum you should be investing for is ten years where you won't be needing the principal. At the historic market return of 10% compounded if you invest $10,000 into the index you should have $20,000 in seven years. In fourteen years, your $10,000 should be $40,000. And in twenty-one years, it will be $80,000. This means that your money doubles every seven years and after twenty-one years, it quadruples! All the while there is only a 25% tax on the 2% dividend portion of your investments return. Again the government encourages stock market investing by taxing dividend income at a lower tax than earned income. This can be done with fees at 1/10th of the 1% that most portfolio managers charge. Every year by putting $10,000 in, you could have $80,000 twenty-one years later. To show how much 1% fees cost, let's assume the index for the next twenty-one years only grows at 7% compounded. At the end of twenty-one years, instead of $80,000 you will have about $43,000. You can see that taking 1% adds up to a tremendous difference over twenty-one years. The 1% fee will not be as large as the 3% illustrated here but over twenty-one years, it is still quite substantial.

Luck is not an investment strategy. Buying the market is. I hope you'll follow my advice, maximize your investment in a good index fund, check your ego at the door, and forgo the compulsion to buy into whatever Jim Cramer and his friends are shouting about on TV on any given day.

You'll thank me one day. Who knew that simplicity, not complexity, was the hallmark of smart investing?

Now *you* know. So take my advice, keep it simple, and enjoy a financial life second to none.

Made in the USA
Monee, IL
07 July 2026

56544278R00079